TRUSTED ADVISORS

KEY ATTRIBUTES OF OUTSTANDING INTERNAL AUDITORS

RICHARD F. CHAMBERS

SPONSORED BY

The Institute of
Internal Auditors
Dallas Chapter

The Institute of
Internal Auditors
Houston Chapter

IIA-Toronto Chapter

INTERNAL AUDIT
FOUNDATION™

"Chambers hits the mark again! *Trusted Advisors* is insightful, thought-provoking, and a must-read for all auditors. This book is about the future of the profession in real time."

MICHAEL J. FUCILLI, CIA, CGAP, CRMA, QIAL, CFE
Auditor General
Metropolitan Transportation Authority

"The wisdom and intellect that Richard has gained from his illustrious career and experiences confidently sparkle through this intriguing book on being 'Trusted Advisors.' No doubt that all levels of auditors will be captivated by the attributes needed to traverse the journey to audit greatness—the nine attributes categorized into three domains are indeed on point and will certainly instill inspiration into the riveting world of internal auditing."

JENITHA JOHN, CIA, QIAL, CA (SA), SEP
Chief Audit Executive
Firstrand Bank – South Africa

"In *Trusted Advisors*, Richard distinctly outlines our role as advisors to stakeholders. The book is highly applicable in today's developments within internal audit where trusted quality and added value are dominant drivers for success. I highly recommend you read it!"

JOHN BENDERMACHER, CIA
Chief Audit Executive
ABN AMRO Bank

"By sharing the elusive attributes of trusted advisors, Richard Chambers shines a light on what separates 'good' from 'great' internal auditors. A definite must-read for internal auditors looking to be part of strategic conversations within their organization."

SALLY-ANNE PITT, CIA, CGAP
Managing Partner - Pitt Group
Chair-Professional Responsibilities & Ethics Committee

"Trust is a two-way street. Not only does the internal auditor constantly assess stakeholders; stakeholders assess whether the internal auditor can be trusted. Richard Chambers sets out in *Trusted Advisors* what the 'right stuff' is to be trusted and how to get there. Essential reading for every internal auditor."

MARK CARAWAN, PHD, CIA, QIAL, CFIIA, ACA
Chief Auditor, Citigroup
Chairman, IIA Financial Services Guidance Committee
and former President and Chairman,
IIA United Kingdom and Ireland

"The pinnacle of success within the internal audit profession is not only becoming a trusted advisor, but also trusting your stakeholders in return. Nobody is better suited to share the necessary skills and experiences required to achieve this goal than Richard Chambers. *Trusted Advisors* is a must-read for internal auditors and business professionals alike."

BRIAN CHRISTENSEN
Executive Vice President,
Global Internal Audit, Protiviti Inc.

"Richard's insightful and clearly organized observations are as relevant to 'up-and-coming' auditors aspiring to leadership positions as they are to experienced CAEs looking to further enhance their effectiveness."

MIKE JOYCE, CIA, CRMA, CPA, FAHM
Vice President, Chief Auditor & Compliance Officer
Blue Cross Blue Shield Association

"In *Trusted Advisors*, Richard has carefully researched the essential attributes that internal auditors should possess to earn the highest level of respect and trust within their career. Certainly a recommended reading for current internal auditors and business professionals alike, but should be considered required reading for future generations of internal auditors."

FRANK M. O'BRIEN, CIA, QIAL
President
Internal Audit Foundation

"When it comes to influential leaders within the internal audit profession, Richard comes to mind as one of the most influential people I know. This book contains insightful information for anyone looking to get ahead and stay ahead."

PAUL SOBEL, CIA, QIAL, CRMA
Vice President/Chief Audit Executive
Georgia-Pacific LLC

"Richard continues to share his long-term experiences and insights on becoming trusted advisors, a concept that leads to success, high reputation, and recognition by our stakeholders. The book outlines nine key attributes that hit the mark and are attributes that internal auditors around the globe can assimilate into their career!"

ANGELA WITZANY, CIA, QIAL, CRMA
Head of Internal Audit
Sparkassen Versicherung AG, VIG
Chairman of the Board
The Institute of Internal Auditors

Published by the Internal Audit Foundation
1035 Greenwood Blvd., Suite 401
Lake Mary, Florida 32746, USA

Cover design by Faceout Studio.

ISBN-13: 978-0-89413-981-9

22 21 20 19 18 17   1 2 3 4 5 6 7 8 9

CONTENTS

I dedicate this book in memory of Joe Plunkett and Ernie Gregory—two of the most inspiring trusted advisors I've encountered during my career.

Early in my career when I pursued a brief hiatus outside of internal audit, Joe had the confidence in me to make the transition from internal audit to the complex field of operations research analysis. He was my boss and mentor, and eventually became a lifelong friend. His death in early 2016 was a huge loss personally, and I miss him immensely. He constantly impressed upon me the importance of striving for excellence in everything I pursued.

Ernie Gregory was one of the most charismatic leaders I have ever known. I worked under his leadership for almost half of my internal audit career. Ernie taught me the importance of saying what you mean and the courage to fight for what is right. His death in 2015 was a huge blow for all of us who knew and were inspired by him.

Any success I have enjoyed, I attribute it to their mentorship over the course of my career.

FOREWORD

By Patty Miller

DURING MY TENURE as chairman of The Institute of Internal Auditors'
(IIA's) Global Board (2008–2009), my theme was "Recognized. Trusted.
Valued." I chose this theme because I felt we needed to challenge complacency in our profession. Being recognized and known in an organization
wasn't enough. We needed to gain the trust of management and the
board, essential to ultimately being valued as a true asset to the organization. For many, gaining respect as a trusted advisor is still an elusive
goal. Yet, it is core to the concept of a professional internal auditor. In
Trusted Advisors, Richard Chambers has chosen to tackle this fundamental topic—in an instructive and helpful manner.

I originally met Richard in 1998 when I worked for Deloitte &
Touche, LLP, and he was working as the assistant inspector general
for the U.S. Postal Service. During this time in our respective careers,
we participated on The IIA Standards Board, where we redrafted
the *International Standards for the Professional Practice of Internal
Auditing* to fit the recently released Professional Practices Framework
(PPF). The Standards Board comprised respected, experienced, senior
practitioners from around the globe and a variety of organizations. Yet,
Richard stood out. He immediately impressed me as a consummate
professional: knowledgeable, articulate, experienced, and informed.
He was a good listener and open to the views of others—critical attributes in bringing cohesiveness and focus to often heated discussions

surrounding the "redo" of the *Standards* at the time. It was clear he had broad experience and knew a lot about how to effectively execute a valued internal audit function.

Fast forward a few years to early 2008 when I served as senior vice chairman of the board at The IIA, challenged with finding a new chief executive who could run The Institute and steer it through significant financial challenges. Our country was experiencing a great recession. People were losing their homes because the housing bubble burst, massive layoffs were the norm, and any unnecessary spending was curtailed. The country's economic fallout directly impacted The IIA—The Institute was facing losses, layoffs, and operational challenges. As senior vice chairman, I led the executive search committee that looked for a new IIA leader who would "stop the bleeding," help recover from economic damage suffered, and restore confidence in The Institute's objectives and stability. Richard Chambers was the first person who came to mind. The entire search committee agreed he seemed to be someone who had the business acumen to solve the financial challenges, but also someone who could serve as a trusted advisor to the staff, our members, and our stakeholders. We completed a professional search and, ultimately, Richard was offered the role of president and CEO. As projected, Richard pulled The IIA team together, solved the immediate financial challenges, and positioned The Institute for the future successes we have enjoyed under his leadership.

One of the attributes I respect most about Richard is his ability to be a direct, transparent communicator in a very fact-based manner. During this challenging period, his ability to clearly communicate helped to rebuild trust. He gave a realistic picture of the financial and operational situations, proposed solutions, kept the executive committee informed, inspired and led his team, and met commitments. Did the executive committee see Richard as a trusted advisor? Absolutely!

Over the years, I've had the pleasure of collaborating with Richard many times on committees and task forces, and feel fortunate to call him a close friend. He seems to inherently know how to modify his style to work best with whomever he's advising. But what Richard knows inherently, he has offered to explain to the rest of us in this book. He gives excellent examples of how to approach different situations, how to advise effectively, and how to gain a reputation as a trusted advisor.

Richard is well-positioned to tackle this topic, given his wealth of relevant experience working in senior audit and investigative positions in government and in professional services serving large global internal audit organizations; meeting with key global stakeholders from boards, regulators, and legislators; and, of course, leading The IIA in representing, guiding, and leading the profession. He has seen true trusted advisors and those who fall short, and heard firsthand from key stakeholders what their expectations (and the gaps) are.

Throughout this book, Richard shares his insights on nine attributes he believes are required to gain recognition and respect as a trusted advisor; to be set apart from others in the profession and held in high esteem. He shares stories and practices to make the nine attributes he explores real and understandable, while also acknowledging that for all of us, this is a challenging journey and perfection at all attributes will undoubtedly elude us all.

I highly recommend *Trusted Advisors* and predict this book will be required reading for all CAEs, whether they have many years of experience or are just rotating into the internal audit department. It will also prove helpful to emerging internal audit leaders within any type of organization. I commend Richard for taking time to craft such a timely and beneficial tool for the profession.

—PATRICIA K. MILLER, CIA, QIAL, CRMA, CPA, CISA
Partner (Retired)

ACKNOWLEDGMENTS

WRITING THIS BOOK has been yet another rewarding experience in my own professional journey. As with all of my professional endeavors, this book would not have been possible without the encouragement and support of so many members of my family, friends, and colleagues. My wife, Kim, continues to be an extraordinary source of support and encouragement. Her words of advice, reassurance, patience, and understanding over the past 30 years have been instrumental to any success I have had in earning the trust of those I served. My mother, Mildred Chambers, continues to inspire me. She taught me at an early age the importance of treating those around me with love and respect. My talented and beautiful daughters, Natalie McElwee, Christina Morton, and Allison Chambers, and their families are more important than any professional legacies that I could ever leave.

Thank you to The IIA's Dallas, Houston, and Toronto chapters for sponsorship of this Internal Audit Foundation publication. I will be eternally indebted to Jane Seago for all of her help in organizing the draft manuscript. She understood my vision for this project and brought boundless energy and an extraordinary writing style to the project. Thanks to Lillian McAnally, my editor, whose award-winning expertise and time in organizing *Lessons Learned on the Audit Trail* rendered her as my editor of choice for this project. Once again, her help on this project and polishing the manuscript was invaluable. Words cannot express my gratitude to John Babinchak, Robert Perez, and Doug Anderson for the talent and enthusiasm they each brought to the writing and editing process. Thanks also to Lori Ondecker and Bonnie Ulmer for their help in making sure the book cover would have the appropriate look and feel.

Thanks also to Jim Pelletier, Marie Lilly, and the entire IIA Audit Executive Center team for their help in organizing and launching the survey that served as the basis for much of the manuscript. Thanks also to Patty Miller, all of the CAEs who participated in the AEC survey, and the men and women who agreed to be interviewed for the book.

Finally, I would be remiss if I didn't thank the countless men and women whom I have had the privilege of calling colleagues over the course of my 40-plus-year career. They have inspired and challenged me to strive for excellence. I learned much from them about the attributes needed to secure and retain trust, and many of them served as role models in my own quest to be a trusted advisor.

ABOUT THE AUTHOR

RICHARD F. CHAMBERS, CIA, QIAL, CGAP, CCSA, CRMA, is president and CEO of The Institute of Internal Auditors (IIA), the global professional association and standard-setting body for internal auditors. With more than four decades of internal audit and association management experience, he has held various leadership roles in the private and public sectors.

Prior to joining The IIA, he served as national practice leader in Internal Audit Advisory Services at PricewaterhouseCoopers (PwC). He also held positions as inspector general of the Tennessee Valley Authority (TVA); deputy inspector general of the U.S. Postal Service; and director of the U.S. Army Worldwide Internal Review Organization at the Pentagon. Currently, he serves on the Committee of Sponsoring Organizations of the Treadway Commission's (COSO's) Board of Directors, the International Integrated Reporting Council (IIRC), and The IIA's Board of Directors.

He has received numerous awards, including being named by *Accounting Today* as one of the "Top 100 Most Influential People in Accounting." The National Association of Corporate Directors (NACD) has named him one of the most influential leaders in corporate governance since 2013. In 2016, the American City Business Journals' *Orlando Business Journal* honored Chambers as a top CEO of the Year. He authored the award-winning book, *Lessons Learned on the Audit Trail*, which is currently available in five languages.

INTRODUCTION

TRUST **IS DEFINED** as "the firm belief in the reliability, truth, ability, or strength of someone or something." For a small word, it packs a big punch.

Over the centuries, great minds from Euripides to Shakespeare have opinioned on trust. More often than not, the concept is awarded great value—something to be earned, something to be shared with caution, and something that once broken is difficult to repair.

Yet trust is one of the most underused words in the internal audit vocabulary. Sure, internal auditors occasionally speak of trust when considering whether they can rely on documents and assertions by management and those they audit. Those in the profession ponder whether they can trust management's intentions, and whether management can be trusted to be forthcoming and transparent during an audit engagement. We even use the clever phrase "trust, but verify," made popular by revered former U.S. President Ronald Reagan. Of course, he was alluding to reducing nuclear warheads, not to the accuracy of documents and assertions presented by those we audit.

So while we use the word *trust* on occasion, it is usually in reference to whether we can trust our stakeholders and those we audit. Rarely do we speak of whether *they* should trust *us*, and rarely do we view trust in the same lofty and vaunted ways as do philosophers and playwrights. Why should that be the case? Shouldn't our stakeholders have "a firm belief in the reliability, truth, ability, or strength" of internal audit?

Shouldn't those we audit trust that we understand the business and will not simply be wasting their time over the course of the audit?

Shouldn't they trust that we have good intentions and do not approach our roles with preconceived notions or bias? Shouldn't they trust us enough to embrace our insights, recommendations, and advice?

Internal auditors speak increasingly of the need to be *trusted advisors*. This is a tall order when we consider the meaning of the words, but I believe it is an attainable goal. Yet very little has been written or conveyed about what that means and how that status can be achieved.

BEING TRUSTED

I explored the concept of trusted advisor a few years ago in my first book, *Lessons Learned on the Audit Trail.* In that book, I reflected upon the salient lessons I learned over my 40-plus-year career in the internal audit profession. During this period of reflection, I also talked to a global cadre of successful internal auditors who confirmed my experience: opportunities to gain and lose trust are infinite in number and variety, and they always cast long shadows.

As you can imagine, given the length of my career and the insights offered by my helpful colleagues, there were many useful, meaningful lessons to report. Recently, however, I found myself increasingly focused on one overarching lesson that came out of the research I did for my first book. Just as metadata is data about data, this is a metalesson—a lesson about lessons. I have come to believe that *what* internal auditors do—although very important—is not as important as *how* they do it. Success in internal auditing is rarely about the obvious activities; instead, it is about who and what the internal auditors are.

I remain convinced that the term *advisor* encompasses the full spectrum of an internal auditor's work, from providing consultation and advice at the request of management to generating recommendations for corrective actions as the result of an assurance engagement. In the end, I believe we are advisors in our professional roles every day.

But, I don't believe that outstanding internal auditors enter the world fully formed, with all their attributes intact and firing on all cylinders. Outstanding internal auditors—like outstanding lawyers, teachers, artists, and doctors—are made, not born. Mastering skills is a long, arduous process, and it is one that true professionals dedicate themselves to at every step in their careers. No one stumbles into greatness. Indeed, part of becoming a trusted advisor is having the "right stuff."

HAVING THE "RIGHT STUFF" TO BE TRUSTED

Some chief audit executives (CAEs) long to be regarded as trusted advisors because it reflects the faith that management has in their advice on pertinent issues. It also lends credibility to their assurance and advisory work, based on their objectivity and profound understanding of the business. I believe that becoming a trusted advisor involves not just *what you know* (risk, control, and governance expertise) but also *how you get things done* (relationship acumen). Both are valuable attributes for internal auditors to possess, but it is only through their combination that one can truly become a trusted advisor.

I've witnessed two internal auditors perform similar actions with very different outcomes. I suspect the reason is that the less effective internal auditor is strong in one trait and deficient in the other. Perhaps he has a strong technical background in internal auditing but can't communicate in a way that resonates with others. In fact, he may just be painful to work with. Or maybe he is a delightful lunch companion—humorous, charming, talkative—but with very little of substance to say. Excellence requires a balance of technical and soft skills.

Internal auditors who rise above challenges and obstacles have achieved that balance by building a broad portfolio of complementary traits and attributes. These select few are not infallible—no one is perfect—but most do find success, and when they don't, they learn from their mistakes, avoid repeating them, and move on.

I imagine most of you reading this would agree with me up to this point. Yes, there are certain traits that successful people in any profession possess. No argument there! Where we might fail to see eye to eye, however, is when we try to outline what those traits are.

Over the course of my career, I've invested a lot of personal resources to researching what traits and attributes make an internal auditor valuable to the organization. I've spoken on the topic, written blogs about it, and collaborated with colleagues on research reports. The organization I lead, The Institute of Internal Auditors (IIA), has conducted a number of surveys on the topic, asking members what traits they think contribute most directly to their success.

While I admit that my opinions have not necessarily remained fixed over time, certain traits and attributes have consistently dominated my thinking and the comments of others. Those attributes formed a list I felt I could champion.

This list articulated the essential building blocks of outstanding internal auditors. It was the raw material that, when closely examined, revealed hidden interrelationships that imbued them with additional meaning. Being an internal auditor, I needed to connect the dots to better understand how these attributes fit together to fashion the very best professionals in my field. I needed data to ensure I was capturing a consensus view of what it takes to be an outstanding internal auditor—a trusted advisor.

It was this impetus to validate that list with data and the material that resulted from that effort that afforded me the confidence to write this book. My goal was to impart not only my own experience, but to aggregate the knowledge of my colleagues around the globe and share that collective expertise with you and future generations of internal auditors.

CHAPTER 1

KEY ATTRIBUTES OF TRUSTED ADVISORS

IT WAS NEVER my intention to write yet another entry in the already-crowded field of books promising to boil down complex business issues into a neat and tidy roundup of the "top 10." If business success were as easy as checking items off a list, we'd all be on the cover of *Forbes*.

Before undertaking the important task of writing this book, I asked people exactly what it takes to be an outstanding internal auditor. Working with colleagues, I crafted a survey that was sent to the members of The IIA's Audit Executive Center (AEC) that contained only one substantive question. We outlined my purpose for writing a book on the traits of outstanding internal auditors and then listed 13 pertinent attributes worthy of consideration, asking respondents to rank the top 10 in order of preference. We also asked them to suggest other attributes, if they felt we had missed any, and explain why they thought they were so critical. I was delighted with the response—hundreds of global CAEs took the time to weigh in. Most simply ranked the list, but one-third of them were passionate enough about the subject to make other suggestions or expand on the traits we had listed.

As I pondered the survey results, I also recognized that these attributes are not exclusive to internal auditors—they apply to business leaders in any field. Internal auditors are hardly alone in seeing the need to understand their industry, think critically, behave ethically, continue learning, interact effectively with others, and engage in the other attributes outlined in this book. The examples I describe revolve around internal audit, but the broader business context certainly applies. The insights shared in this book are for those seeking to be trusted advisors in virtually any profession.

MAKING SENSE OF THE DATA

I was pleased to observe that the data confirmed my own conclusions and broadened my perspectives on the topic. I now feel comfortable that the resulting list of attributes represents a strong consensus view of the portfolio of attributes outstanding internal auditors share. Ultimately, I discovered a structure that made sense to me: nine attributes in three categories, each critical to success as an internal auditor—and to becoming a trusted advisor.

ATTRIBUTES OF OUTSTANDING TRUSTED ADVISORS

PERSONAL	Ethical Resilience	Results Focused	Intellectually Curious	Open-Mindedness
RELATIONAL		Dynamic Communicators	Insightful Relationships	Inspirational Leaders
PROFESSIONAL		Critical Thinkers	Technical Expertise	

I believe the attributes, as displayed, make sense if viewed in a somewhat linear order, starting at the top and working down. Successful internal auditors must possess the attributes in the personal category and apply them in every transaction—and every interaction—with others. The personal attributes are absolutely essential for internal auditors in achieving success.

Moving down the diagram, attributes in the relational category demonstrate that how a person interacts with others conveys how he or she relates with them. I don't mean to suggest that internal auditors should always strive to be liked. Not everyone is going to like you. In fact, I recall one of my blogs that received the most heated responses offered my opinion that "sometimes internal auditors can be right or they can be liked," but not both. Not everyone agreed with me, but I stand by my statement. However, despite how internal auditors might fare in a popularity contest, they should be respected and recognized for their professional courtesy, objectivity, equitable treatment of others, motivational behavior, and ability to speak and write in a way that accommodates and engages their audience.

Then we arrive at the base of the diagram—the professional category. These are the capstone qualities that help them acquire a seat at the table (multiple tables, really, from the boardroom table to the lunch table in the employee cafeteria—each important in its own way). Thus, they have earned the respect that is essential to apply their professional intellectual abilities and well-honed technical skills to address business issues.

Personal attributes. This category focuses on who internal auditors are at the very core of their being. These attributes are ingrained in outstanding internal auditors. They simply can't achieve excellence in the profession without them.

- Ethical resilience
- Results focused
- Intellectually curious
- Open-mindedness

Relational attributes. This looks at how internal auditors deal with others. Internal auditing is a profession that relies on collaboration and effective interaction with all levels of the organizational hierarchy. It is also an exercise that frequently deals with sensitive issues. The attributes in this category help the internal auditor build a team and obtain the information needed to undertake a successful engagement, report the results in a way that is meaningful to a variety of audiences, and obtain a consensus on critical solutions. Success in these areas depends on building, fostering, and maintaining good relationships.

- Dynamic communication
- Insightful relationships
- Inspirational leadership

Professional attributes. This category looks at the knowledge and skills outstanding internal auditors leverage in their roles as professionals. They must have a deep understanding of the business of their organizations and the industry in which their organizations operate if they are to offer credible assessments and solutions. Internal auditors have a number of tools that help them get their work done. There are computer-assisted audit techniques, frameworks, standards, guidance— and the list goes on. But it takes certain skills, contained in this category, to understand how, when, and why to use those tools. The best decisions are based on an ability to analyze the problem, identify and evaluate potential solutions, consider the environment, and only then proceed.

- Critical thinking
- Technical expertise

Looking at our diagram from the top down, and considering it in the most simplistic terms, we can conclude that outstanding internal auditors are effective within themselves, within their communities, and within their jobs. Just like business leaders in all professions.

USING THE BOOK

Each chapter in this book examines an attribute in detail, why the attribute is important, and how it's evidenced in the workplace. At the conclusion of the book is a recommended list of resources for readers who wish to strengthen their skills in these attributes. I would have greatly appreciated this sort of guidance when I was new to the internal audit ranks. Back then, I concentrated extensively on learning the technical skills of the profession—how to develop an audit plan for every engagement, document the results of the audit, and craft a well-written audit report. I certainly don't regret the time I spent polishing those skills; they served me well throughout my career. However, I would have welcomed the information in this book to help me balance the scales, which brings me back to why I wrote this book.

We can't just show up, articulate our views about future risks, and expect people to heed our advice without first earning their trust. Neither can we expect them to respond favorably to our assurance work.

Let's say you write an audit report in which you identify deficiencies and offer recommendations for remedial action—recommendations on which you believe the report's readers should take swift action. They are much more likely to do so with greater commitment if they trust you, believe that you know what you are talking about, and consider the work you do to be sound, fair, and objective (as opposed to doing so only because corporate policy requires it or the audit committee is breathing down their necks).

I hope readers around the world will use this book as a path to becoming trusted advisors and to make an impact on their organization—a goal I believe most internal auditors aspire to achieve. I hope they use it as a guide for self-analysis and introspection and a source they can use to benchmark themselves and validate their professional strengths and the areas that need improvement.

What I *don't* want to happen is for readers to start thinking of their shortcomings and come to the conclusion that they are inadequate in their roles. People can't excel at everything, but they can still find ways to be effective as they progress.

The book can be especially useful for CAEs by identifying not only the traits they should model but also those they should be looking for when building their internal audit teams. Knowing which attributes outstanding professionals share should prove quite useful when preparing position descriptions and interviewing candidates.

STARTING THE JOURNEY

Like other professions, internal auditing is populated by practitioners with a broad range of skill and commitment levels. The traditional bell curve is in play. A small percentage of internal auditors are on the left end of the curve, representing those who are not well suited for the profession or have not made the commitment to be so. The vast majority of internal auditors fall in the middle of the curve, doing the job quite competently. And the remaining few are on the right end of the curve, where the truly outstanding professionals reside. This book is about them and the shared attributes that make them outstanding internal auditors. They have always inspired me, and I hope learning more about what makes them tick will inspire others to start their own personal journey to the right side of the curve.

Becoming an outstanding internal auditor takes years of experience, ongoing training, and an awareness of emerging trends in the professional environment. Most of all it takes passion. I've been fortunate to know a lot of outstanding internal auditors during my more than four-decade career. Invariably, they bring to their role more than just expertise, although that is certainly important. They bring a sense of enthusiasm and commitment that separates them from the crowd. They truly believe in the contribution internal audit makes and take great pride in being part of that good work. They become change agents in their organizations, their work is impactful and generates value, and their performance acquits the internal audit profession well in the eyes of stakeholders. They are true masters in the field.

We should never abandon our aspiration to continue to grow, improve, and strengthen ourselves. In his book, *Good to Great: Why Some Companies Make the Leap...and Others Don't*, Jim Collins opened a lot of eyes by describing the many small but consistent ways the companies he and his team studied moved themselves from mediocrity to consistent outperformance of the market. These companies studiously avoided the usual "big bang" approaches to try to inspire change. They didn't capitalize on (or create) a crisis, nor did they conduct a formal and splashy campaign, complete with taglines and logos, designed to rally the troops. Instead, these companies undertook very pragmatic and consistent processes focused on achieving excellence in small, attainable, and sustainable chunks. They adhered with unfailing discipline to a companywide framework to keep employees—from top to bottom—on track with the plan. They built their success day by day.[1] Making progress on building outstanding attributes requires a similar approach: slow, steady, unflinching, and goal-focused.

PERSONAL ATTRIBUTES

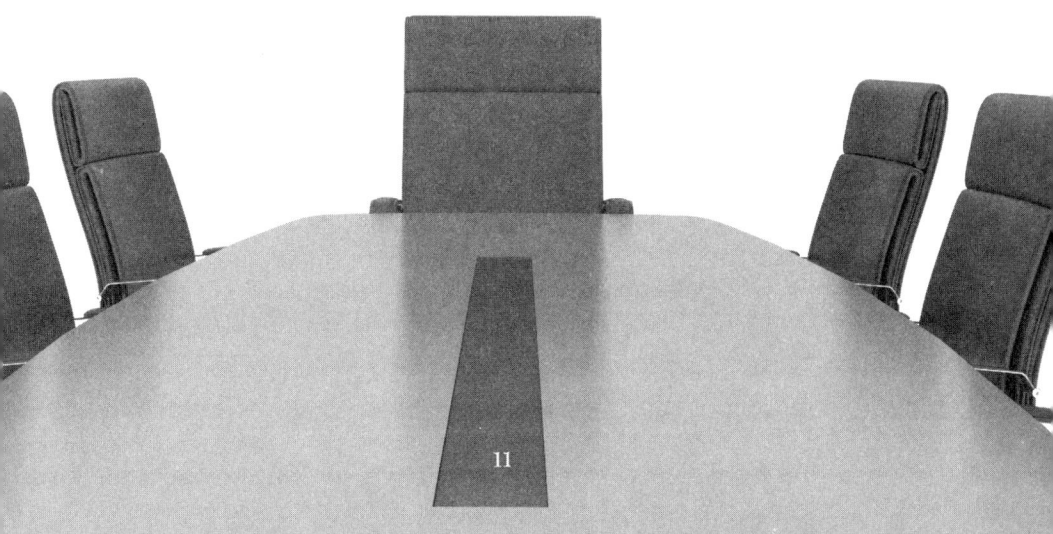

CHAPTER 2

ETHICAL RESILIENCE

I ENJOY WATCHING football (that is, American football, not soccer). Sometimes during the game, when an infraction is committed before the play begins, the referee will throw a penalty flag. The flag often signifies a false start if certain players on the offensive team move before they're supposed to. At times, there are referees who either ignore the infraction or are passive about making the judgment call.

Internal auditors who sit on the sidelines and fail to call out ineffi-ciency, waste, fraud, or mismanagement are spectators. More commonly, internal auditors are referees, observing the plays that make up the normal course of business operations and blowing a whistle or throwing a yellow flag when circumstances warrant. They are objective in assessing whether a foul or infraction has occurred, but they are in reactive mode— responding to what took place in the past.

The most effective internal auditors are those with enough fortitude to blow the whistle *before* trouble ensues. They see troubling issues in the formation stage, raise a concern, and take a stand to ensure things are done right. But, as I discovered years ago, there has to be a high degree of trust between internal auditors and those whom they are cautioning about pending wrongdoing or calamity. Without trust as a basis for engagement, the conversation can become awkward or even polarizing.

Ethics is an area that plays a significant role in my view of out-standing internal audit performance; so much so that I decided to feature ethical resilience as my first area of focus. I've been known to characterize ethics as "table stakes" for those wishing to engage in internal auditing. It's a strong statement, but I stand by it. Internal auditors can't accomplish their mission without a diligent, unceasing commitment to ethical behavior.

Larry Sawyer, an iconic internal audit author, wrote about the importance of trust in ethical behavior. He wrote, the "key to any profession is the trust placed in it by its clients." Everyone knows how important ethics are; that's a foregone conclusion. But I believe that, for internal auditors, ethical behavior is so critical, it goes beyond just a commitment. Outstanding internal auditors do more than just commit to ethics; they model ethical conduct in everything they do by being resilient, even when the ethical position may not be a popular stance. They may be tested ethically, but they withstand the challenges to their ethical convictions and bounce back stronger than ever. That's a lot to express in one word, which is where metaphors are helpful.

Obviously, the CAEs who responded to the AEC survey agreed with this view. More than half of them selected ethical commitment as one of the top three traits shared by successful internal auditors.

Reinforcing that viewpoint, the Internal Audit Foundation's Common Body of Knowledge (CBOK) 2015 Global Internal Audit Practitioner Survey asked CAEs around the world to rate themselves on their perceived level of competency on 10 core competencies, with 1 being "novice" to 5 being "expert." The survey data indicated that CAEs rated themselves highest in ethics (4.3 overall),[1] which validates my point that ethical resilience is a top attribute for outstanding internal auditors.

Paul Sobel, vice president/CAE for Georgia-Pacific LLC, states it very simply and powerfully: "In our role as auditors, ethics and integrity are the foundation for our ability to provide objective assurance, advice, and insights. In essence, it's the foundation for our credibility."

Sobel shared an incident in which his ethical conduct had decidedly unexpected consequences.

> "At a previous company, I was auditing an executive's expenses and there were some inconsistent charges. After further investigation, including review of his work emails, I determined he was defrauding the company.

The amounts were relatively small, but when talking to the CEO, I recommended termination of the individual as I didn't see how he could be fully trusted if he was expanding his expense account. The head of HR and Legal were also in the room, and they weren't sure termination was the best answer. However, the CEO agreed with me and the individual was terminated.

There is a happy outcome to this. Some months later, the executive emailed me and thanked me for helping him understand that what he was doing was wrong. He had found a new job and 'turned over a new leaf,' which he said was largely due to how professionally I handled my investigation with him."

His unwavering commitment to ethical behavior within the company had a positive impact on the employee and saved the company from fraudulent actions that could have cost them in the long term.

COMMITTING TO ETHICS

As the leader of a global organization that requires compliance with a formal Code of Ethics to serve as a member or hold a certification, I have an unwavering commitment to behaving ethically. At The IIA, we don't skirt the issue; we believe internal auditors must stand for what is right, adhere to the highest ethical code, and never yield to pressures to bend the rules. An ethical lapse by one internal auditor can undermine trust not only in that individual but also in those around him. The higher in the organizational chart the transgression occurs, the more damaging the potential impact. We in the profession must share a commitment to ethics. For the most part, I believe we do.

In most organizations, the internal auditors are perceived as being far more likely to disclose ethical misconduct than to act unethically themselves. But we are human. I will never forget my surprise and disappointment when I viewed the results of a survey of 70 CAEs attending an IIA event a few years ago. One-third of the respondents acknowledged that they had "discovered or witnessed unethical actions" within their own internal audit functions.

Making the effort to clean our own ethical house is important not only in the context of what internal auditors do in their everyday jobs, but also in their role as business leaders. In her book, *7 Lenses: Learning the Principles and Practices of Ethical Leadership*, Linda Fisher Thornton says getting employees to act ethically is largely driven by their desire to "follow the leader." If they see top management behaving ethically, desiring to serve others, and making a positive difference, they are inclined to respond in kind.[2]

Organizational commitment to ethical behavior is not just a matter of hosting an "ethics day" or showing a slide presentation during new-hire orientation, although all efforts at communicating expectations relative to ethics are valuable. The most impactful things leaders can do to influence employees are subtler: openly discussing ethical gray areas, acknowledging the complexities that can arise in work situations, treating ethics as an engrained way of behaving, celebrating displays of ethical conduct, showing respect for those with different opinions and difficult personalities, and expecting everyone to meet ethical standards.

These behaviors (at any rank in the organizational chart) should not be difficult. If we think of ethics as a way we interact, collaborate, and create synergies with others, it should be natural to act ethically and expect the same behavior from others.

The results of such behavior can yield unexpected results. Early in my career as a CAE, the chief financial officer (CFO) asked my internal audit team to perform an audit. He had a strong personality and was sure the company was being billed for purchases it didn't make. He wanted my team to find evidence to support his belief. I sent the internal auditors to conduct the audit, and they found no evidence of transgression, which put me in a bit of a tight situation. The support from the CFO and other executives was important and necessary to me, yet I knew that audit results weren't what he wanted to hear. By telling him he was wrong, I risked losing both his fledgling trust in the internal audit department and his willingness to use us for future projects, but I knew I had to be straightforward with him. As expected, he did express some disappointment that we didn't validate his concerns.

Not long after that, he called me to ask my team to do some work in another of his functional areas. After I expressed our willingness to do so, I told him I was surprised he had contacted me for an additional project since I didn't give him the news he wanted to hear the last time. He responded that my honesty in those circumstances proved to him that my team and I would be fair and objective and he could rely on our work. I don't think he intended our first encounter to be a litmus test, but it was. Once your stakeholders have a chance to check your ethical compass and confirm that it's pointing true north, they know they can follow you because you won't lead them in the wrong direction.

ETHICAL BEHAVIORS

No one is saying that exercising ethical behavior is easy, but maybe half the challenge is in agreeing on exactly what constitutes ethical resilience. In the AEC survey, we used the following terms to elaborate on what we meant by ethical commitment, and I suspect few would argue with their inclusion:

- Integrity—being known for strict adherence to high moral principles
- Courage—being brave enough, even in the face of professional or personal danger, to do the right thing
- Honesty—displaying unwavering commitment to dealing in truth
- Accountability—taking responsibility for our actions and the resulting perceptions
- Trustworthiness—building a history of ethical behavior that forms a foundation upon which people can place their trust

Courage especially seems to be a factor in ethical behavior. A number of the survey respondents ruminated on the importance of courage. Take the following comments, for example:

> "Inner courage: to follow leads, to follow your gut belief, to professionally confront management and the board, to raise the questions few people want you to raise, to put it all on the line (in terms of taking the risk to do what is right)."

"Courage: the ability to express one's opinion and give advice even when the ideas are not popular or wanted."

"Courage to stand alone, if needed, when tough issues need to be raised to management and the board."

Courage is what drove Bethmara Kessler, CAE of Campbell Soup Company, to select ethical commitment as one of her top two choices in the AEC survey. She explains that courage is a particular challenge for auditors because in her long experience of managing audit teams, she has seen internal auditors sometimes waver in their defense of difficult findings for a variety of reasons: they, like most humans, want to be liked; they want to avoid difficult conversations; they feel the pressure to serve too many masters with competing needs; and they fear their actions may hinder their future career opportunities in the business. But, she remarks, "We have to remind internal auditors that courage is important and they should step forward when they see something. Look at Harry Markopolos, who tried multiple times to break open the Madoff scandal. He just kept going back to the SEC [U.S. Securities and Exchange Commission] over and over to make his point. I'm sure it was not an easy thing to do. It took a lot of courage. In my view, he's a hero."

Another internal audit hero who deserves notice is Heidi Lloce Mendoza, currently undersecretary general for the United Nations Office of Internal Oversight, and before that, commissioner and officer-in-charge of the Commission on Audit (COA) of the Philippines. Mendoza came to the world's attention as a result of a 2002 audit her team conducted that uncovered massive bid rigging by former Makati City Mayor Elenita Binay. Mendoza served as a government witness in some of the antigraft cases filed against the former mayor. In response to her speaking out against the former mayor's corruption, Mendoza's home was broken into multiple times and she was the target of threats that required special security protection. Yet, despite her admission that she was still being harassed about her role in the corruption trials 13 years after the fact, when she resigned from the COA in 2015 she indicated that her passion for her work had not abated and she felt "no pain, no trace of regret"[3] for her experiences.

I met Heidi Mendoza in 2016 when she delivered opening remarks to The IIA's Global Council in New York. Her remarks that day directly addressed the importance of ethics, and she noted that internal audit professionals need to stand together to bolster each other in the face of adversity spawned by doing the right thing. She noted that "internal auditors should never be alone when they have to stand and tell the truth." She went on to challenge the profession to "work together to become the conscience of society." Most of us will never have to face a situation in which our ethical commitment results in threats of bodily harm, I am grateful to say. Internal auditors like Mendoza provide us with role models for living our beliefs even in the face of extreme pressure.

Joe Martins is chief of internal audit for Citizens Property Insurance Corporation, a state-owned property insurer in Florida that operates under a strict no-gift policy required by state statute. The employees cannot accept even a bottle of water from a supplier or a notepad from a vendor's booth at a conference. He points out that in such an environment, it is easy to make a minor mistake, but even the slightest slip in a government entity can elicit unfavorable public opinion driven by negative press—a combination that tends to have a long and unforgiving memory. "In this environment, one really needs courage to stand by what is right," he explains. "And when something goes wrong, discipline must be consistently fair and everyone needs to be held to the same standard of accountability."

Honesty was also emphasized by several AEC survey respondents as a critical component of ethical commitment, noting that honesty should not be restricted solely to interactions with others. An occasional good, hard look in the mirror is often called for. As one respondent stated, internal auditors need to have "a willingness to challenge assumptions—even their own."

Surely honesty is a given in any list of desired ethical behaviors. There can be no ethics without honesty. But sometimes it seems that people believe honesty can only be served with large side dishes of bluntness and insensitivity.

Instead, I suggest that internal auditors (and all business leaders) make regular, sincere use of empathy. Internal auditors are often required to deliver difficult, uncomfortable messages. There is no avoiding it. But tempering honesty with empathy enables them to deliver those messages with sensitivity to the other person's concern and priorities. It's not only basic kindness; it also makes receiving the messages more palatable and more likely to be considered constructively.

WIRED FOR INTEGRITY?

All of this discussion about how and why to behave ethically seems so obvious. How could anyone fail to see and understand the appropriate ethical actions to take in any situation? Most people inherently want to be good, so behaving with integrity should be second nature, right?

Not always. There are many reasons why people may fall into an ethical lapse in the workplace, including:

- Divided loyalties among the senior executives
- False belief to protect the organization at any cost
- Fear of missed career opportunities
- Conflict of interest or cowardice
- Professional blind spots (i.e., no longer capable of being objective)

Some examples of blind spots that internal auditors consistently fall victim to include "These policies really aren't good anyway," or "It's not worth damaging a personal relationship," or "Better no external quality assessment than a bad one." In these instances, the people involved may truly think they are doing the right thing by sidestepping an ethical response to a given situation. Not only is that not the case, it is the first step onto a slippery slope. As Paul Sobel points out, "Unethical behavior typically starts with something small that can be rationalized, and then grows from there."

We have a right to expect integrity from everyone we work with regardless of their title or responsibilities, but there is no question that some professional roles are more likely than others to run into situations requiring difficult ethical decisions. I strongly believe internal auditing is one of those professions. I have often said that internal auditors should be beacons of ethical light in every organization and inspire utmost, unquestioning trust. But we are subject to at least the same pressures (cultural, political, and organizational) as everyone else in the enterprise.

SHATTERPROOF THE HOUSE

Actually, I think internal auditors have a tougher challenge than many others in the organization. It's challenging to sustain a reputation for objectivity over the long term when we live and work in the same environment in which we perform our audit responsibilities—sometimes for a few years, sometimes over an entire career. Everyone is watching internal audit all the time to see if we are walking the talk. Joe Martins calls us "example setters for an organization" and recognizes that we are "constantly assessed by the groups we audit." I call it having a target on our back. If internal audit is not following organizational policies, or just *appears* to not be following policies, the fallout will affect trust in the department and every internal auditor in it.

No one expects internal auditors to be flawless, because we're human after all. But if the flaws cause others to question our ethics, we've lost a significant advantage that will likely undermine our ability to be perceived as trusted advisors. If management is aware of even minor ethical transgressions, their response when we offer advice or recommendations at the conclusion of our engagements is likely to be, "Why should I listen to him? He takes vacation days without charging them," or "She filed a faulty expense report and had to reimburse the company." Internal auditors cannot afford the luxury of being vulnerable. Our behavior must be above reproach if we are to provide counsel to others. And don't be surprised if, the first time you call out a senior manager for a serious ethical infraction, suddenly every minor infraction you ever committed is thrown back at you.

Neither can internal audit afford to fail to live up to its commitments. Michael Rosenberg, managing director and CAE at Och Ziff Capital Management, points out that internal auditors have to understand that they have a commitment to both the firm they work for and a broad, diverse group of stakeholders. "We have to walk a fine line, understanding the firm's needs, the board's needs, management's needs, and investors' needs," he explains. "If we're not trustworthy, and if the people we work with aren't trustworthy, we leave the door open to fraud."

I believe most internal auditors can stake a claim to consistently act with ethical conduct. But occasional lapses do happen, and when they do, they often make the news. Many reading this book will likely recall reading about certain high-profile cases. The actions of unethical internal auditors constitute a massive betrayal not only of their employers and former colleagues but also of their profession. Internal audit has many responsibilities, one of which is ethical overseer. In that capacity, like Caesar's wife, it must be above suspicion.

To look at it another way, we have all heard the common wisdom that those who live in glass houses should not throw stones. But sometimes as internal auditors our job is to toss a rock or two. So if we're going to throw stones—and, of course, we are—we'd better make sure our own house is shatterproof. A steadfast commitment to ethical behavior coupled with a strong and effective quality assurance and improvement program will help ensure we avoid flying glass.

Bethmara Kessler believes one way to shatterproof the internal audit function is to ensure the right people are in it. She elaborates, "I want people on my team who keep the shareholders and the reputation of the company, rather than their own career, at the top of their mind. Some of what we do makes us not the most popular people in the organization, but we have to do it. We need to go about our business with courtesy and grace. My goal—and the goal for my team—is to be firm, fair, and friendly."

THE POLITICAL PRESSURE COOKER

Ethical issues are rarely black and white. Gray areas abound. It's not always clear what the internal auditor's moral obligation is to speak out if there are issues relating to a company's products, a manufacturing process, or a third party's practices. Our responsibility to identify fraud, inefficiency, risk management failures, or control deficiencies may not align perfectly with our obligation to our employer's profitability and shareholder value. We must engage in ethical decision-making not only to protect the organization from potential reputational damage, but also because it is the right thing to do.

Effective CAEs learn how to navigate the political waters even under intense pressure from others within their organization. As part of their research for their book, *The Politics of Internal Auditing*, Patty Miller and Dr. Larry Rittenberg surveyed nearly 500 CAEs worldwide on the political pressures internal auditors face. They also conducted interviews and focus groups to gather data and insights into first-hand experiences of remaining ethical even when the CAE was in the political hot seat. The results of their research were very revealing:

More than half of the survey participants (55 percent) had been subjected to pressure to omit or modify a finding; the vast majority (71 percent) noted the pressure was due to a concern that the report would reflect badly on key operating management.[4]

As part of the research project, Miller and Rittenberg also conducted interviews with 23 CAEs, representing a mix of public, private, and governmental organizations. Among the personal traits that rose to the top were:[5]

- Courage
- Strong ethical compass
- Excellent communication skills
- Professionalism
- Calmness
- Personal integrity
- Fair-minded
- Leadership

Note that second on the list is strong ethical compass.

In my long career in internal auditing, I have been challenged on my own ethics, and it is something I have never forgotten. Years ago while working at the Pentagon, I had started volunteer work for The

IIA. As part of that volunteer activity, I attended a meeting at The IIA's global headquarters in Florida. On my way back, I stopped in Georgia to attend a football game. This time off was my personal time and I paid for the trip using my own resources. However, someone highly placed in the Pentagon discovered I had gone to the game and suggested to my boss that I had attended the meeting just to go to the game. I had discussed my plans thoroughly with my boss well in advance and had his approval. When he was faced with this allegation, he took strong exception and explained the facts to the accuser. He also told me about the allegation so that I could be prepared should any related issues arise later.

The allegation was entirely unfounded, but it taught me something about perception and its aftermath. I had to retain a relationship with my accuser, and I won't deny that it was a struggle to put his allegation out of my mind and maintain objectivity in dealing with him. I'm happy to say I succeeded, but the fact that I still recall the details 25 years later is proof that the lesson has never left me. The people with whom you have a contentious issue today are the ones you may be auditing tomorrow, so you must learn to compartmentalize these individual episodes and not allow them to affect your unbiased attitude. The incident was also the first time I noticed that target I mentioned earlier firmly affixed to my own back.

We all walk around with baggage; our perspectives are colored by our experiences. We have to leave the baggage at the door with every audit. We must have a firmly fixed moral compass. We can't make deviations for expediency's sake. We can't take shortcuts. That doesn't mean we shouldn't seek flexibility and try to find alternative paths to a satisfactory conclusion. But we can't allow our quest for flexibility to cause us to compromise ethical principles. We can try to understand the moral challenges of others without accommodating or excusing them.

Maintaining ethical resilience is not often the easiest path, but it is one on which we must remain steadfast. Our ethical stumbles not only damage our own professionalism, they chip away at the reputation of our profession as well.

Ethical resilience is a trait that not only provides value in and of itself, it also supports the other traits mentioned in this book. Having a firm grip on our own ethical beliefs clears away some of the clutter that can distract us from focusing on desired results.

CHAPTER 3

RESULTS FOCUSED

BARELY A CENTURY ago, internal auditors were typically found only in the railroads and other early twentieth century industries, and even those internal auditors were primarily focused on whether receipts and disbursements were being properly handled.[1] The steady progress over the past century has shifted internal audit's focus from examiners to advisors focused on operations, technology, and strategy. Internal auditors in the twenty-first century must bring a strong and unwavering focus on results, and outstanding internal auditors engender trust on the part of their clients that they will do precisely that.

Outstanding internal auditors are motivated by analyzing data, leveraging technology, and providing actionable advice, all while remaining scrupulously ethical, independent, and objective. There is no way to accomplish all that without an unyielding focus on results and an unwillingness to let go of a project or problem until we know that the desired results have been fully achieved. Frankly, I think results orientation must be one of our superpowers.

That is why I am disappointed when I see a business article that casts even a slightly negative light on results focus. This negative connotation arises from the binary spin that has been put on the concept: the notion that a focus on results requires us to give up more desirable traits, such as empathy, nurturing, and team building. The implication is that we can achieve stellar results, but only at the expense of trampling over people as we cross the finish line. I believe that is a false choice.

BLACK AND WHITE

As I mentioned in chapter 2, in relation to ethics, real-world issues are seldom black and white. Life would certainly be much easier if everything were so distinctively labeled. Choices would be clear-cut. But as it is, we have to deal with some fairly nuanced situations and often must select from the lesser of two evils—or the greater of two goods. How and why has orientation on results become exempt from this basic fact of life?

Somewhere along the way, business leadership was cast into a series of either/or choices. In this view, leaders either:

- Focus on results *or* on people
- Emphasize tasks *or* employees
- Use hard *or* soft skills
- Favor results *or* processes

The drawback to this viewpoint is that it places the two options (results versus people, hard skills versus soft) on opposite ends of the spectrum, not allowing them to coexist. In my experience, I strongly believe that one cannot be achieved without the other.

Imagine trying to achieve results without empowered, motivated, well-trained, and dedicated people. Or ask yourself, "How much progress could I make toward my business objectives if my interactions with my employees, managers, and peers consisted entirely of an unrelenting focus on the task at hand, never tempered with an occasional chat about the family vacation or the hometown sports team?" Try to picture a way to achieve results without well-designed, well-tested, and well-executed processes.

To me, the conclusion any reasonable person would reach by doing this exercise is clear: success is achieved by tossing aside the binary view of focusing solely on one aspect to achieve results and embracing all the factors that contribute to attaining it.

There is research to support this view. In 2009, 60,000 employees were surveyed to identify how different characteristics of leaders combined to affect employee perceptions of great leadership. Results focus was one of the characteristics offered for evaluation on the survey. Social skills was another. The employees rejected the binary view entirely. If a leader was perceived as being very strong in results focus, only 14 percent considered that leader to be "great." The percentage was even lower (12 percent) if the leader was considered strong in social skills. However, when the two characteristics were combined—the leader was perceived to be strong in both areas—72 percent of employees surveyed classified that leader as "great."[2] Obviously, these 60,000 employees didn't see results focus in terms of either/or. Rather, they saw great leaders as those who not only focused on the ends (results) but also those who recognized how crucial the means were (social skills).

Mark Rosa, vice president of internal audit for Houghton Mifflin Harcourt, certainly sees the value in the duality of traits when he states, "Internal audit departments need our internal auditors to have the core technical skills and education. But what I am finding even more important over time is people's passion for the work, interpersonal and communication skills, and strong work ethic. If you don't have these inherent characteristics, the technical skills tend to be less relevant."

WHAT CONSTITUTES RESULTS?

For internal auditors, a good result isn't simply a matter of finishing an audit and writing the report. Obviously, those two tasks are important to doing the job, but internal auditors who are truly results focused care about much more:

- What happens after the report is delivered?
- Did the audit have an impact?
- Did it create productive and beneficial change in the organization?
- Did it identify opportunities for improvement?

Or if the objective of the audit was to affirm compliance with regulations or policies, did it do so—and did it recommend appropriate corrective actions that should be taken to remediate any noncompliance so it doesn't happen again? Outstanding internal auditors care more about outcomes than outputs. They understand that the outcome after a report has been generated is more meaningful than the length of the report itself or the number of findings and recommendations cited in the report. Quality over quantity. An internal auditor's mission is not truly complete until management acknowledges the recommendations and implements them, and the recommendations produce positive outcomes. As Charlie Johnson, general auditor of the Lower Colorado River Authority, points out, "It's hard to say we're adding value if people just read our reports and file them away. Our organizations need to be able to say that our work compelled them to move in a direction that validates and supports strategy or to fix things that impeded progress in that direction."

If internal auditors perform their work well and are good at what they do, they should rarely surprise operating management. The results may surprise executive management, which may nurse a misplaced confidence in how well the enterprise is operating. But the managers who are closest to the design, implementation, and management of controls in a functional area often recognize the challenges they face. As a manager once said to me, "I don't need someone to come in and tell me I have problems. I know I have problems. I need someone to come in and tell me how to fix them." Being results focused means recognizing that the audit doesn't exist only to point out problems—management often already knows about them—more importantly, it provides solutions. As I used to tell my staff, "If our findings only consisted of conditions, then we should just call ourselves inspectors." It is our ability to identify the causes and offer recommendations that management can implement to address the conditions that truly set us apart. The most accomplished internal auditors I have known recognized that the end result was not the report; it was making things better for the good of the company.

It should come as no surprise that I believe this focus on results among outstanding internal auditors is a key ingredient in becoming a trusted advisor. Realizing results, as defined here, depends on management's trust in the individual's work quality and insights.

FOUNDATIONAL SUB-TRAITS

The CAEs who were interviewed for this book frequently assigned sub-traits, such as discipline and drive, to results orientation. Perhaps more than any other attribute examined in this book, a dedication to results is dependent on a mastery of a variety of sub-characteristics. Out of the AEC survey emerged a list of sub-traits that undergird the attribute of being results focused. Among them were:

- Productivity
- Strong work ethic
- Balance
- Resilience
- Persistence
- Determination
- Timeliness
- Leadership
- Perspective

It would be hard to argue how any internal auditor could be considered outstanding, or become a trusted advisor, without consistently demonstrating every one of those foundational sub-traits.

Nearly 88 percent of the CAE respondents recognize that a laser-like focus on achieving results is a critical attribute to success. The head of internal audit for a major natural resource company echoes the correlation between being results focused and being viewed as credible and trustworthy, especially because internal auditors must "understand the governance system and be a role model in complying with it." He notes the amount of discipline and drive it takes to consistently demonstrate exemplary work and the frequency with which temptations arise to divert our focus from desired results. In his view, a lack of consistent focus leaves internal auditors open to a reputation for "preaching water and drinking wine."

Many of the CAEs pointed to sub-traits such as resilience, persistence, and determination as critical to achieving a results orientation.

One noted the need for tenacity in the face of obstacles, and another described the usefulness of tenacity in working through difficult scenarios to develop a balanced solution that meets the needs of multiple stakeholders. Similarly, one survey respondent explained that great internal auditors need to have enough conviction in their ideas to pursue an item until the answer is found. If that's not a focus on results, what is?

Perseverance is a concept closely related to persistence and resilience. In the context of being results focused, I think it's worth considering, especially in relation to dealing with a setback. Nobody is immune from experiencing failure at some point in their lives. No one makes it through life or a career without the occasional run-in with things not working out as intended. What matters is *how* you deal with it. Some let it derail their hopes and plans, never quite recovering. Others learn from adversity, resolving to grow and emerge wiser and more proficient. That's being results focused at its best—not letting a temporary setback impede progress toward the desired result.

Work ethic is another concept mentioned in the survey responses, and it's one that especially speaks to me. I believe everyone has an internal flame that ignites their passion. That flame comes from a different place for each of us. For some, it was instilled in us by our parents during childhood. Others find it through faith, an inspiring mentor, or athletic competition. When our flame is lit, we're fired up to get the job done and pursue excellence. Outstanding internal auditors live with the flame on high, consistently compelled to do their best work. They could transition into other professions and the results would be the same. A strong work ethic drives them to excellence.

Of course, a results orientation is a positive trait only when the results are aligned with and support an organization's strategic objectives—a distinction noted by several AEC survey respondents. One said that effecting positive change, making a difference, and contributing to the organization's overall success are strong motivators for many internal auditors. In essence, these motivators *are* the results upon which they are focused. Another specified the importance of commitment to the organization's objectives and mission. In his view, this connection focuses the internal auditor on the risks and needs of the business. Otherwise, he notes, "it's just an academic exercise."

Timeliness is also a contributed factor to being results focused. Some internal auditors are so slow in conducting their audits that the results are too late to be meaningfully applied. Meanwhile, the audit client becomes frustrated and dissatisfied with the internal audit function and may be hard to bring back into the fold. Other internal auditors are too speedy, failing to gather enough information or analyze it closely to support their recommendations or missing a critical issue. I often refer to these as "drive-by" audits. Then, when the client's careful review of the recommendations proves them to be faulty, it undermines internal audit's credibility. In neither case did the desired results—a careful, professional, thorough, and helpful audit—receive the appropriate amount of focus.

Another element I consider essential to being results focused is leadership. Good internal audit leaders can instill or fan that internal flame I spoke of earlier, but they cannot do it alone. Good leaders need good followers—those who are open to motivation. When I was new to the internal audit field, I had the seeds of results orientation within me, but that inclination was not necessarily focused effectively. My boss at the time was not results focused, so I didn't have a role model to follow. Instead, I channeled my energy in other ways—pursuing further education, even doing some teaching. Those were worthy activities and I don't regret them. But I recognize now I should have been directing more energy into investing in my career. Once I fully found my passion for the profession, I worked wholeheartedly toward defined results. I suspect that if I had a results-focused leader then, I would have made the transition earlier and more expeditiously.

Leadership is also important in this context because its absence may cost the profession some of its future outstanding internal auditors. Without results-focused leadership in internal audit, I left the department to pursue a career in operations research analysis (cost analysis). After three years, I was tapped by the organization's CEO to return to internal audit as the CAE. I came back with a single-minded commitment, but other young auditors who don't have the benefit of a results-focused leader may direct their energies into another profession permanently.

Anyone who follows sports has seen instances of an individual or team absolutely loaded with talent but unable to perform as expected.

This, of course, is largely a coaching failure. No one is focusing and directing that talent. The same is true in business. A company may have wall-to-wall superstars, but if there is no results-oriented leader keeping everyone motivated and on track, the bottom line will reflect a consistent inability to meet expectations.

PUTTING THINGS INTO PERSPECTIVE

Several CAEs also mentioned perspective as a sub-trait—one worth considering in more detail. One of the survey respondents declared, "It's a killer when it's lacking," and I have to agree. Internal auditors who deliver reports with insignificant findings or conclusions will have an uphill battle in gaining the trust of their clients and others within the organization.

If we want to be results focused, then we need to put things in perspective and "work smarter, not harder." That's easier said than done. But as internal auditors, we can spend a lot of time reviewing files, generating documentation, creating workpapers, and cross-referencing and indexing reports. That's part of what we do, after all. The problem is that these activities are not necessarily generating desired results, unless they are focused on critical issues or significant risks. One survey respondent perfectly captured the outcome of a disproportionate focus on this sort of busywork: "Making a mountain out of a molehill is a fast track to losing management's confidence."

Some internal auditors find themselves in the grips of the terrible compulsion to achieve perfection. It's an especially common shortcoming among new internal auditors who have the noble goal of producing perfect work. They want to conduct one more interview, expand the sample, or do another walk-through—whatever it takes to produce the perfect outcome. We may admire their intentions, but perfection takes time, and time often undermines the ultimate value of an internal auditor's work. As noted in *Lessons Learned on the Audit Trail*, sometimes never is actually better than late.

When we develop a sense of perspective, we can define what is critical to generate desired results (high-impact auditing) and what is fluff. Doing risk-based audits—focusing on the areas of greatest risk to the organization—and leveraging technology are two ways internal auditors can ensure their eyes are fixed on the big picture and not on the trivial details.

Another CAE noted that perspective supports the ability to turn theory into practice—a skill that is critical to achieving results. In this individual's view, too many internal auditors are unable or unwilling to develop solutions that are fit for purpose, instead hiding behind theoretical best practices or idealistic controls. Outstanding internal auditors have a profound understanding of best practices and processes, but they do not demonstrate a slavish devotion to them. They recognize that circumstances should be reflected in the drive for results.

WHEN THE FOCUS BLURS

What happens when the focus on results begins to waver? Or isn't broad enough in scope?

The head of internal audit for a major natural resource company points out that results focus, in the sense that we seasoned internal auditors might define and value it, is not necessarily a motivator for younger generations. The millennials are famously characterized as being more interested in sustaining a balance between career and personal life than in dedicating what they consider inordinate amounts of time to work. In his view, "We failed in the past to acknowledge that the young generation becoming auditors has different career perspectives and needs." He worries that if we don't adjust our focus on results and accommodate the desires and needs of the coming generations, we risk losing new talent. He adds, "That's why focusing on results without understanding the motivations of the people delivering the results is wrong."

Mark Rosa relates a story about a staff auditor who started her job with plenty of "book smarts" but no relevant audit experience, no certifications, and no accounting degree. However, she was extremely motivated and results focused. He describes her energy, her willingness to turn over every rock, her innate curiosity, and her persistence—all of which combined to result in a high-profile report that got management's attention and added true and tangible value to the enterprise. However, according to Rosa, "The flip side of this individual is what I see much more often—people with all the certifications, all the prestigious degrees, but who just don't want to do what it takes to succeed in the job. That's where a good portion of my turnover comes from and it appears to be fairly common in the profession."

My view? I think we sometimes fail in being results focused when we don't take a true risk-based approach in defining our audit plans for the year. We risk spending significant amounts of resources (i.e., time) and ending up with insignificant results. This sense of "spinning our wheels" may be part of the reason younger generations or those interested in becoming internal auditors lose interest and abandon the profession. During the mid-2000s, I observed many internal audit departments in the United States were heavily focused on Sarbanes-Oxley related work that was not risk-based. Younger internal auditors were hearing from their counterparts how tedious and unrewarding it was to test an overabundance of financial reporting controls. As a result, when applying for a position, many internal auditors new to the profession were blunt in saying they would not be interested if it included extensive Sarbanes-Oxley work. Not all results are created equal, and those in low-risk areas should take lower priority to those in high-risk areas. Charlie Johnson echoes these thoughts: "We can be doing a great job of auditing things exceptionally well, but if we're not auditing the right things, we're not adding value."

Most of us are probably familiar with the anecdote about apologizing for sending a long letter because there wasn't time to write a short one. This sentiment translates well to internal auditing. If we had unlimited time and resources, we could look at everything and give almost absolute assurance of what the problems are, or that there are no problems. None of us lives in that world. Outstanding internal auditors know that achieving focused results requires seasoned professional judgment. We use appropriate tools, such as risk assessments, to know where to focus, when to dive deeper, and where there are likely to be results that can drive change.

I believe another area of risk related to results orientation is in being so keyed in on the desired results that we miss some of the steps that must be taken to get there. This may be more prevalent among internal auditors with several years of experience. We may go into an audit thinking we already know how to address issues that may arise or the results we are likely to find by the end of the audit. That mindset can be a direct route to embarrassment or failure. Outstanding internal auditors never assume, and they maintain a very healthy respect for failure. They also recognize that the most likely way to add value is to discover something not previously identified. As the saying goes, "If you always do what you have always done, you will always get what you have always gotten."

Ultimately, those who are results oriented are known for being so because it's reflected in their personal brand and they work hard to sustain it. They don't want to let people down. If their stakeholders know they are good internal auditors and expect them to perform accordingly, they will do what it takes to rise to the challenge, not only for themselves, but for their department and organization.

DRIVEN TO RESULTS

About halfway through my career, I had the unique opportunity to help build a large audit function from scratch. The U.S. Postal Service had never had an inspector general function until the late-1990s. I was tapped by the new inspector general to assist her in assembling an audit team capable of auditing one of the largest organizations in the world. In less than three years, we hired hundreds of auditors—many of whom were seasoned in identifying fraud, waste, abuse, and mismanagement.

Hiring so many auditors in such a short period of time was extraordinarily challenging. Each brought his or her own experiences, habits, personalities, and characteristics to the new organization. As with any new hire, it wasn't always evident how they would fare until they stepped into their new role. What was fascinating to witness was how quickly some adapted to the new organization and environment compared to others. Those who were results oriented adapted quickly and made very strong impressions on skeptical managers within the Postal Service. Those who were simply content to get by often undermined the progress we needed to make.

As I reflect back on this "laboratory" that I had a role in leading, I recognize that the results-oriented professionals we hired were not content to simply do their job. They were obsessed with learning about their new organization, immersing themselves in the operational risks and challenges in the areas they audited, establishing credibility with management, and delivering audit reports and recommendations that were embraced and implemented. The results-oriented professionals became impact players and were often trusted by management and viewed as superstars.

Results-focused internal auditors have a keen ability to adapt to stakeholder expectations. After all, they don't achieve results if they give their stakeholders something they don't want or fail to give them what they do want. They know that trust is built and sustained through consistent excellence. They focus their time and effort on what matters and constantly deliver.

A focus on results is a recognition of the importance of the end game. However, good outcomes are possible only when they are based on good information. Sometimes the right information is easy to find, but more often it requires asking insightful questions and a healthy dose of intellectual curiosity to explore an issue from a variety of perspectives.

CHAPTER 4

INTELLECTUALLY CURIOUS

ONE OF MY favorite television commercials features a child walking out of an office building with his father. The child asks, "Hey Dad, who was that man?" His father answers, "He's our broker." From there, the boy peppers his father with a series of questions he can't really answer: "Do you pay him?" "How much?" "What if you are not happy, do they have to pay you back?" At that point the dad answers, "No," and the boy asks, "Why not?" When the dad responds, "The world does not work that way," the boy asks once more, "Why not?" The final image shows a father that is clearly struck by the incisiveness of a simple question. The commercial ends with a woman's voice saying, "Are you asking enough questions about the way your wealth is managed?"[1] Who among us hasn't been a participant in a toddler's repetitive game of asking "why?" As adults, we patiently try to provide a clear and concise reply, only for our answers to be retorted with yet another perpetual series of "whys."

Like children who truly want to understand the world around them, it's desirable to have a healthy dose of intellectual curiosity about your work. Outstanding internal auditors who are not content with a pat answer will continue to probe until they get to the bottom of why something does or doesn't work.

ASKING WHY

Asking "why" is one of the most important and fundamental responsibilities of internal auditors. They want to know what happened, but intellectually curious internal auditors are not satisfied until they know *why* it happened. And they will not relent until they fully understand the root cause of the issue.

As seasoned internal auditors know, the critical elements of an audit's findings typically include criteria, condition, cause, and effect. Condition and effect are often fairly obvious, but that's not the case with cause. Cause is usually ferreted out only by asking "why"—and knowing the answer to "why" is the first step to effecting positive change. Internal auditors cannot make, with any real confidence, recommendations to mitigate risk or prevent a recurrence of an issue if they do not understand why the issue occurred in the first place. When they stop asking "why," it's because they have the final answer. They have arrived at the root cause.

Getting to the bottom of things requires more than just incessantly asking "why," as a child might do. If we did that, our clients would undoubtedly lose patience with us in short order, and our reputation for credibility would suffer. One of the CAEs who responded to the AEC survey characterizes the quest to get at the root cause of an issue as "provocative inquiry," defined as "the knack for asking smart and unsettling questions." Another respondent echoed that sentiment, pointing out that because internal auditors cannot be proficient and/or knowledgeable on every topic, they have to "know what questions to ask."

Maticia Sims, vice president and corporate controller for Blue Cross Blue Shield of North Carolina, has seen the effects of not asking enough questions, asking the wrong questions, or even asking too many questions. She recalls a business partner saying, "We know internal audit wants a seat at the table, but you don't understand our process and you just slow us down." While she recognizes the need for discipline in asking the right questions, she emphasized to her business partner that engagement of internal audit to ensure that risks and controls are considered will help ensure processes are executed as intended. She still encourages her staff not to shy away from probing for information. "My opinion is: Let's ask the questions before we get into crisis mode. Once we're in crisis mode, the time to ask questions is severely limited."

But even asking the right questions is unlikely to provide us the information we need if we don't ask them in the right way. Outstanding internal auditors know they don't have all the answers; the person they are interviewing is the one with the information. Getting that individual to provide the information involves putting him or her at ease by creating a comfortable environment for the interview. This is part of being a trusted advisor: being the kind of person who people will trust enough to share what they know.

I can recall several audits that I conducted or led where individuals sought me out to share perspectives or leads. They trusted me enough to sit down with me and share information that was often sensitive or even damaging to the reputation of their own managers and departments. They believed that, as the internal auditor, I would use the information to generate audit results that would be accurate and yield improvement. Had I failed to listen to them or to investigate the leads or allegations they made, I would surely have lost their trust. And the next time I came into their department, they would have remained silent.

ADDRESSING THE MOST IMPORTANT ISSUES

So far I've been talking about asking the right questions in the context of audit interviews. In reality, internal auditors should begin digging much sooner. Some of the most important questions they can ask, for example, are those addressed to stakeholders when developing the annual audit plan, starting with "What do you believe are the most significant risks or obstacles to achieving the goals and objectives in your area of responsibility," or simply the proverbial "What keeps you awake at night?"

There are benefits to conducting a risk assessment and basing audit plans on those areas of highest risks. This helps us concentrate our resources where we can create the greatest value. In fact, when internal auditors focus their audits on areas that aren't tied to risk, it may be one of the few times that intellectual curiosity can be too much of a good thing. Internal auditors are not the only people with a finite amount of time and resources. Engagement clients have their limits as well. If we waste time chasing the root causes of inconsequential matters, we will likely fail to adequately address the most important issues. And if we try our client's patience through a scattershot approach to auditing, we are sure to wound our credibility and reputation for perspective. One of the most disparaging remarks I can recall hearing about internal auditors in my early years as a civilian auditor for the U.S. Army was "the internal auditors are like a bunch of second lieutenants running around chasing rumors." Ouch!

Another reason intellectually curious internal auditors start their line of questions *before* audit plans are drawn up—besides managing resources wisely—is to ensure full alignment with the enterprise's strategic objectives. The mission of internal audit, as recently updated by The IIA, calls for internal auditors to "enhance and protect organizational value." We will hardly enhance and protect value if we demonstrate that our priorities, as evidenced in our audit plans, are out of sync with our organization's business objectives. Any gap in expectations puts us at risk of becoming irrelevant.

A DOSE OF HEALTHY SKEPTICISM

Skepticism is a concept often used in tandem with intellectual curiosity. Merriam-Webster defines *skepticism* as "an attitude of doubt or a disposition to incredulity either in general or toward a particular object."[2] Some people consider it a survival tactic in today's environment of information overload.

I think it's important to add the adjective *healthy* when talking about skepticism within internal auditing. It is fine to question what appears to be obvious, and it's appropriate to assume that the information, even provided by authority figures, may not be entirely accurate. Questioning enables internal auditors to uncover truths that allow them to make better decisions and form more effective and compelling recommendations. The flip side of this is an unhealthy dose with a veneer of suspicion, which may turn unnecessarily negative or veer into cynicism or inappropriate territory. Unhealthy skepticism does no one any good, even if it is within the context of internal audit. When I first became a CAE, one of my most seasoned internal auditors constantly demonstrated a glaring liability. He seemed to harbor suspicions about almost everything and everyone. His skepticism clearly was unhealthy, and managers and others throughout the organization dreaded seeing him coming. As his supervisor, I mentored him and helped him to recognize how others perceived his skepticism. Gradually, he made improvements.

Outstanding internal auditors have to bring a bit of psychology to the table—a topic that is likely not covered in standard auditing curriculum. They need to understand what motivates people and what their priorities are *today*. In circumstances of extraordinary pressure, good people will do bad things and smart people will do dumb things. For example, a young parent with hungry children and no money for groceries may be moved to commit fraud. Really smart people may start to believe their own press clippings, come to believe they are untouchable, and then make disastrous mistakes. Intellectually curious internal auditors know they can't simply look into someone's eyes and understand their motivations. They have to question. Nor can they think that just because someone might be highly experienced, the individual's word can be taken at face value. They must dig deeper.

There's a reason internal auditors gather several types of evidence: testimonial, documentary, and physical. We don't rely solely on testimonial statements; when possible, we test them against documentary and physical evidence. We know our eyes and ears can deceive us.

During my tenure as a CAE, I can recount many instances when an internal auditor came to me breathlessly professing to have identified fraud or a significant control failure. Yet when we sat down and looked at the evidence, it became apparent that the auditor had impatiently jumped to conclusions. Further audit work often revealed a logical explanation, not fraud or the perceived control failures that were initially suspected. We must remain skeptical to avoid rushing to judgment.

It may seem odd to present the concept of trust in a discussion about skepticism, but balancing those two is a challenge that internal auditors face. For trusted advisors, their intellectual curiosity sparks an innate respect for just how much trust they can bestow. Their success is measured by the level of trust they engender. They know that if they consistently signal mistrust (unhealthy skepticism), as my seasoned direct report did, others might be less inclined to trust and confide in them. That in turn will undermine confidence in audit findings and recommendations. The line between trust and skepticism is not easy to walk. To manage it, trusted advisors have to bring all their interpersonal skills into play.

USING INTUITION

Initially, I hesitated to introduce the word *intuition* here. The term has taken a few hits to its credibility by having been conferred almost magical implications. But it's not an extrasensory perception; it's a natural ability or power that makes it possible to know something without proof or evidence. It usually arises from our subconscious, as we process new information through the lens of our experiences and knowledge. With that understanding of intuition, it's clear to me that outstanding internal auditors are imbued with it as an offshoot of their intellectual curiosity.

Before writing this book, I had a conversation with a colleague about the premise for it and asked him to name an attribute he felt outstanding internal auditors possess. Without hesitation he proposed intuition. It surprised me, but I've since conceived the notion that an internal audit can sometimes resemble a jigsaw puzzle. In such instances, I can imagine having all the pieces laid out in one place, but I have no idea what the picture is. I note that many of the pieces are predominantly blue, and some show bits of birds and brightly colored umbrellas. Through intuition I decide it is probably a beach scene. I confirm that by putting the puzzle together. The same can be true in an audit. Internal auditors sometimes have a lot of pieces (of evidence) before them, and they have to use their intuition to get a strong feel for what they are likely to form. Then they take the rest of the audit from there, pursuing and testing the results of their intuition.

Many years ago when I was at the Pentagon, I was working on an audit of an area dedicated to providing training. Budgets were distributed through the command structure, so the budget for this area was assigned from higher up in the hierarchy. The training area had exhausted its annual budget midway through the year with disastrous consequences, and all remaining training exercises had to be cancelled. I was sent by a higher commander to investigate how the shortfall occurred and to offer recommendations that would reduce the likelihood of recurrence.

I spent two weeks interviewing people and looking at the paper trail, but I was still not sure whether I understood how they ran out of money. I remember sitting in my hotel room puzzling over the countless interviews when I finally connected the dots in my mind's eye. In the previous years, the higher command had given the training area its budget with the understanding that those funds had to last the entire year. However, when the higher command itself got more money partway through the year, it funneled some of those additional funds to the training function. I began to believe this was a case of conditioning. The commander in the training unit had been consistently told at the beginning of every year that the initial budget allocation was all he was going to get, and then every year he would get more about halfway through the year. Based on this tradition, he assumed this year would be the same, so he spent his entire budget in the first six months, only to discover that no additional funds would be arriving that year.

I tested the hypothesis. I re-conducted the interviews, starting with the idea that the expectation of additional funds led to this year's budget shortfall. Sure enough, as I probed further, people began to come clean, as did the training commander. They were making what they considered a safe bet—assuming that the experiences of previous years would recur—but their luck had run out. Skepticism kept me from accepting the initial explanations, intuition prompted me to put together the pieces and develop the hypothesis, and intellectual curiosity led me to validate it through additional questioning.

This story highlights another facet of intellectual curiosity: a complete lack of fear of the uncomfortable. I had interviewed that commander several times, but I couldn't allow myself to fear interviewing him again. When I asked him if he had been spending money because he expected more, I was in essence saying, "You've lied to me all the other times I've talked to you about this because you didn't admit it." I won't deny that it was uncomfortable, but it had to be done.

Outstanding internal auditors must be willing to ask a question again (and again and again), even if they already asked it. If their intuition, curiosity, or instincts don't drive them back to the interview, they won't get to the root of the problem or generate the results they need.

The bottom line is, internal auditors are not doing their job if they don't know why something happened.

LIFELONG LEARNING

As I mentioned before, experience and knowledge are crucial to making the right call. That's why commitment to lifelong learning is not a chore for outstanding internal auditors. They truly can't see any other way to do their job. Their intellectual curiosity compels them to discover new things, understand on a more profound level, and expand their knowledge so they can make useful connections among disparate facts. Like Aristotle, they recognize that "the more you know, the more you know you don't know."[3] And they are determined to remedy that.

Several individuals who responded to the AEC survey noted the need for internal auditors to further their education. One called it an ability to "learn on the fly," citing the importance of quickly understanding new concepts, business models, technologies, etc. Another emphasized having a keen focus on continuous learning and growth to keep up with the profession and stay relevant.

This ties in with Carrie Weber's selection of intellectual curiosity as her top attribute of outstanding internal auditors. "Internal auditors need to have the drive to learn about best practices, industry happenings, and what is going on throughout the company," said Weber, vice president of internal audit for Ameritas. "The more we learn, the more value we can provide. The world around us doesn't sit still. We need to be continuously learning so we can adapt and be relevant to the current business environment and emerging risks."

Maticia Sims considers a commitment to learning especially critical in her environment. Noting the drastic and exceedingly rapid changes in the U.S. health-care industry, Sims said, "My organization is looking to internal audit to really understand the complex issues facing us. As a result, my audit committee and business partners continue to expect more from internal audit—and it's not more of the same. We truly don't have the option to *not* continuously learn, even if we wanted it."

Lifelong learning is one of many ways outstanding internal auditors pursue constant improvement. They ask a lot of questions during audits because they truly want—and need—to know the answers. They want to understand the perspectives of the person being interviewed. Karen Begelfer, vice president of corporate audit services for Sprint Corporation, once worked with an audit committee chairman who always said he was looking for athletes to be part of the audit team. She explained, "Athletes tend to be good at a lot of things. They are eager to learn new areas that will help them in their area of focus, and are certainly not afraid to work very hard to master a new discipline."

She recalls another example of lifelong learning:

> "One of my staff worked in another audit-related department before joining my group. In that department, she had a very focused responsibility: matching the figures from one set of documents to another. When we began to consider adding her to our group, we asked the people she reported to about her performance; they offered rave reviews. She interviewed well and we hired her for an entry-level position. A few years later she is still at entry level, with no real outlook for advancement. Why? She was very good at what she was asked to do, but she had no intellectual curiosity. She did not think in terms of what new skills she could learn to add value.
>
> Conversely, another member of my staff surprised me a few years ago by advising me he had heard of some software called ACL, had downloaded it and was playing with it, but didn't have any data sets to load into it. He thought it might be a useful tool for us, so he wondered if I had any data he could use to further get to know the software. I was thrilled as it was an area we wanted to develop, but we did not have a lot of people with expertise yet. Testing software was not his job; it was not even related to his background, but he had the intellectual curiosity to seek it out and make a self-driven, proactive effort to learn it. Today he is in a management capacity related to audit data analytics."

A willingness to pursue new areas can be extremely helpful for internal auditors. We can never know what new skill or area of professional knowledge may enlighten our future audits. After all, the subject matter expert whom the client needed yesterday may not be the one he needs today.

Internal auditors cannot afford to gain a reputation of being disengaged from the business. We strive for objectivity and independence, each of which requires a degree of separation, but we cannot allow that separation to be perceived as being out of touch with the real day-to-day challenges, opportunities, and our overall business environment. When I was inspector general at the Tennessee Valley Authority (TVA), I took a class on power generation. I didn't have to do the audits there—I had a team of almost 50 auditors to do that—but I felt it was important that I understood what TVA did, how it happened, and what core processes were involved. I did the same thing at the U.S. Postal Service. I wondered how a piece of mail got picked up in Florida and delivered in Alaska three days later, so I did the research to better understand the core processes involved in moving the mail. Within two years I was testifying before congressional committees on the efficiency and effectiveness of postal operations. I am not unique; there are outstanding internal auditors who make the commitment to understand, on a nuts-and-bolts basis, what their organizations do—whether it's manufacturing heavy equipment, serving meals, providing higher education, delivering government programs, or offering investment advice.

Ken MacLeod, director of internal audit for NAV CANADA, also supports the need for internal auditors to remain curious about issues and technologies that can affect their company. He gets regular emails and RSS feeds from news organizations, professional organizations, and consulting firms covering emerging topics and other organizations' experiences. "It is a great way to identify topics that may require further research," MacLeod said. He recalled when cloud computing was new and his employer was assessing its applicability. While the pros and cons were being evaluated, MacLeod wanted to make sure that the risk assessment was comprehensive. "I used multiple sources to summarize various aspects of cloud computing that could impact the company," he said. "This helped to broaden the discussion. While there were training courses available, no one course would have been able to cover the breadth of information I was able to access on my own."

When Carrie Weber accepted a position with a new company, she needed to understand the core business quickly. She undertook a rigorous exercise of learning as much as she could from every source she could identify. It paid off. "Building the knowledge of the business and the company helped put me in a position to better lead my team, be credible with the business, and be seen as a trusted advisor," said Weber.

REIGNITING OUR INTELLECTUAL CURIOSITY

What if we, as internal auditors, wake up one morning and find our personal beacon of intellectual curiosity has gone out? Is it time to hang up our audit plans? Probably not, but it may be time to shake things up a bit. If we've become a little too comfortable doing audits of financial controls, maybe we should do some audits in operations. Or if we've been focused on audits of operational controls, IT audits may be in order. Our intellectual curiosity can be reignited when we force ourselves into unfamiliar situations. If we've done something so long that we know the answer to "why" before we even ask the question, it's time to transport ourselves to a place where the answer will surprise and amaze us.

It's hard to imagine why anyone would question the need for intellectual curiosity in internal auditing—or in any profession, for that matter. But consider this: we live in an extremely complex age that gets more complex by the day. For example, some experts predict that by the year 2020, data production will be 44 times greater than it was in 2009. It is impossible to hide from complexity, so we better learn how to deal with it. Internal auditors, who must take on a deep understanding of the business functions of all the departments they audit while maintaining a firm grasp on audit skills and honing their soft skills, have a special need to know how to create order out of chaos.

Writing for *Harvard Business Review*, Tomas Chamorro-Premuzic, CEO of Hogan Assessment Systems, a professor of business psychology at University College London, and a faculty member at Columbia University, said three elements must be present to manage complexity effectively.[4]

First is the intellectual quotient (IQ), which refers to mental ability. Because IQ enables people to learn and solve problems more quickly, it has a positive impact on real-world outcomes, such as job performance and objective career success.

Second is the emotional quotient (EQ), the ability to perceive, control, and express emotions. Why would this help in dealing with complexity? People with a higher EQ are less susceptible to stress and anxiety; they are more effective in their interpersonal skills, so they are more successful at handling corporate politics; and they tend to be entrepreneurial, which renders them more innovative, proactive, and comfortable with taking risks.

But the third reason is especially germane to this chapter. It is the curiosity quotient (CQ), described as having a "hungry mind." People with a high CQ are more inquisitive and open to new experiences, they find novelty exciting, and they generate original ideas. They can deal with complexity effectively because they tend to be more tolerant of ambiguity and nuance, and they are likely to expand their knowledge acquisition over time. Knowledge and expertise often have the result of translating complex situations into familiar ones, making them easier to solve. Chamorro-Premuzic calls CQ "the ultimate tool to produce simple solutions for complex problems."[5]

It turns out that being smart isn't enough to deal with today's complex issues. Being empathetic and sensitive isn't enough either. It takes those things combined with an equal dose of intellectual curiosity to cut through complexity and get to the heart—the root cause—of problems. As Ken MacLeod says, "Relying on intellectual curiosity is the only way I have been able to stay on the leading edge of the curve, if not ahead of the curve." Sounds like a lot of outstanding internal auditors I know.

Exercising our intellectual curiosity is bound to turn up new information and innovative ideas. And part of intellectual curiosity is having an open mind to receive and accept ideas that show merit, even if they are new to us or don't align with the beliefs we have always held to be true. Open-mindedness is a necessary companion trait to intellectual curiosity, as we will explore next.

CHAPTER 5

OPEN-MINDEDNESS

A FEW YEARS ago, a joke about internal auditors was making the rounds:

> **Question**: How many internal auditors does it take to change a light bulb?
>
> **Answer**: It depends. How many did it take last year?

Naturally, the joke brought a smile because, for many who heard it, there was a faint ring of truth. Many of our stakeholders see internal auditors as creatures of habit who are comfortable with the routine of how and what they audit. Obviously, in the real world, many internal auditors are open to change and make recommendations that will improve the efficiency and effectiveness of their client's operations. But the truly outstanding internal auditors I have known thrive on change. They enthusiastically seek out opportunities to make quantum improvements in their approach to audit and the solutions they identify when their audits identify risk management or control deficiencies.

OPENING THE MIND

When I first joined the internal audit profession more than 40 years ago, the process of compiling an annual internal audit plan, undertaking the various engagements, delivering the reports to the auditees, and ultimately conducting a follow-up audit was incredibly routine. Our findings and recommendations were often very predictable, frequently cut and pasted from one audit to the next. Management was unlikely to disagree with our recommendations because, after all, those same individuals had agreed with the same findings and recommendations year after year.

Innovation and open-mindedness were often not expected nor desired by those in internal audit leadership roles because they too had become creatures of habit. However, in the twenty-first century, we operate in a dramatically different environment.

Internal audit's approach once focused on hindsight, which was useful in the past and is not entirely irrelevant now. Then the focus broadened to include insight, a highly innovative vantage point that's also still important. Now we live in a world that's very future-focused, and if we're not capable of articulating how risks might play out beyond the horizon, our value as internal auditors will be limited.

Today's environment requires internal audit to have a much more open and creative approach to its work than just a few decades ago. As Aileen Madden, head of corporate audit & advisory at Air Canada, explains, "With the increasing expectations that internal audit must respond to, it is not okay to remain status quo anymore. If you raise the bar one year, you are expected to continue raising it, and the only way to do that is to be creative in how you perform and report on your work."

Like all professionals, internal auditors must recognize that change is inevitable. No matter how effectively an organization operates, change can emerge from any direction. But outstanding internal auditors are not threatened. They are receptive to new information, new ideas, new techniques and tools, and new solutions, no matter where they originate. The days of the buttoned-down internal auditor are gone. Today's top practitioners are open-minded, unafraid of change. In a world that requires auditing at the speed of risk, internal audit cannot afford to be otherwise. Trusted advisors aren't reluctant to "audit at the speed of risk" out of fear of the "risk of speed."

Lars Christensen, vice president and chief internal auditor for Canadian Western Bank, knows the importance of being open-minded. Indeed, he considers it the top attribute of outstanding internal auditors. He explains, "I believe that to really add value to our organizations and 'get a seat at the table,' we have to demonstrate that we are more than just risk and control experts." Christensen recognizes that times have changed since the days of checkbox auditing, and he points to the need to think innovatively and provide an opinion on strategic and operational issues—traits that might have been seen as outside internal audit's domain in the past.

Ultimately, a reputation for open-mindedness will resound with others. Stakeholders will perceive it as being flexible—a trait that one of the AEC survey respondents defined as "positively reacting to changing/stressful conditions." Flexibility, in turn, positions internal audit as being reasonable. Open-mindedness, flexibility, reasonableness—each builds on the other, culminating in credibility. Best of all, they move us ever closer to trusted advisor status because you must be seen as credible before you are seen as incredible. As noted by Aileen Madden, "Being open-minded and demonstrating that we are reasonable and flexible go a long way in building trust and being seen as a trusted advisor."

EMBRACING CHANGE

What does open-mindedness look like at work? How do we recognize the characteristic in ourselves and in others? Unlike most other traits I discuss in this book, open-mindedness may be the most difficult to observe in action.

Of course, the most obvious display of open-mindedness is revealed in how a person deals with diversity—that is, diversity of thought, rather than the traditional categories of gender, ethnicity, religion, or sexual orientation. People may see exactly the same situation or evidence, yet they have an entirely different perspective on it. Outstanding internal auditors are willing to recognize that diversity of perception and not only seek out what others may have to say, but also give it thoughtful, unbiased consideration and, when appropriate, factor it into their own thinking on the matter. Rob Gould, director of internal audit at Harley-Davidson Inc., says every audit encounter must be approached with an open mind. He shares an example from the early years of his internal audit career, illustrating the fact that open-mindedness does not equate to indecisiveness or an unwillingness to stand your ground.

"I was assigned to audit a plant outside the United States. My boss's view was that this plant had serious control issues and I would find numerous and complex problems. The management of the plant, on the other hand, thought everything was running smoothly. I performed the audit using my customary approach of asking a lot of questions and listening carefully to the responses. I did end up finding issues, but they were not nearly as serious as my boss expected me to find. They were, however, more serious than the plant's management expected, and the reaction was fairly emotional. I was in the middle, getting pushback from both sides. I worried about my relationship with my boss and the relationship I had carefully built with the plant's management. Ultimately, because I had taken an open-minded approach to the entire audit, I felt comfortable that I had done a thorough and objective audit that weighed all perspectives and my findings were sound. I told my boss that I was the one on the ground, I was the one who had spoken to the people and had seen what they dealt with every day, and he would just have to trust my conclusions. That is exactly what happened. The audit went well and relationships were strengthened on all sides."

"You don't work in that area every day, you don't know everything about what they do, you can't know in advance why issues exist," Gould notes. "You have to listen carefully and let them know their opinions and concerns are being heard. And you must communicate back with objectivity and consistency. The clients may not agree with everything you say, but they must believe you are unbiased. Otherwise you have no credibility."

Open-mindedness can be deeply challenged by change. Rather than simply being open to change and riding it out, outstanding internal auditors are typically agents of change. They create buy-in, motivate action, maintain momentum, and establish a sense of urgency even when management may have other priorities. If you believe, as I do, that internal audit can bring about positive change, you must embrace change not only in what you do but how you do it.

This ties in with stakeholder expectations, which have shifted over time. Boards and audit committees now expect internal auditors to follow the risks. So when new risks emerge or old risks rear their ugly heads (and they do regularly), their expectations of us transform accordingly. As I noted in *Lessons Learned on the Audit Trail*, our stakeholders ultimately judge our value. I would also add that it is our stakeholders who will ultimately decide the extent to which we are trusted advisors.

Being open to change enables us to have a hand in choosing what we want change to look like. That is pretty powerful stuff, but it doesn't come without a significant threat—complacency. The minute we become complacent and think we know everything there is to know about internal auditing, the risks we audit, and feel we no longer need to invest in learning and growing, we cease to be an outstanding internal auditor or an agent of change. And we will certainly never step into or sustain the role of trusted advisor.

PRODUCTIVE FAILURE

Perhaps I am an optimist, but I believe most people are born naturally open to new ideas, experiences, and people. You only have to look at how children interact to see that. They don't immediately see people or ideas as good or bad. They eagerly approach each other at play time, snack time, even nap time. They are freely, even gleefully, open to new experiences and the other children with whom they are sharing those experiences. Sadly, this natural receptivity to new ideas may be one of many childhood traits we lose over the years.

Like many characteristics, open-mindedness can become easier with practice, though some may shy away from it because they fear failure (a lack of open-mindedness in itself). The good news is that recent research reveals there are benefits to be gained from experiencing and overcoming failure.

In a study at the Learning Sciences Lab of the University of Singapore,[1] researchers set up a situation in which the subjects were sure to fail: they were given an extremely difficult math problem to solve without any instruction or assistance. As expected, the group was unable to solve the problem, but they did generate creative ideas about the nature of the problem and what a potential solution might look like. Those ideas led them to perform better on problems posed later in the study. The term for this is "productive failure," and as the name indicates, it implies that it is okay, even desirable, to struggle with something (like learning open-mindedness) before mastering it.

Experiencing productive failure is crucial to an internal auditor's growth, but I will alleviate it somewhat by pointing out a few things I know you should *not* do, behaviors that might actually undermine your efforts to become open-minded. Most of these I learned through my own beneficial struggles, so consider them a bit road-tested.

Don't dwell on the past. How likely is it that people will seek your advice if you tell them only how things used to be done? They may find the information interesting from a strictly historical perspective, but ultimately they need help knowing what to do right now, in six months, or next year. If you're not able to envision what the future looks like from your client's point of view, your client won't view you as a valuable resource. Over time we have seen many innovations that enable internal audit to adapt and maintain or become more valuable. Technology is a good example, because it multiplies our capacity to an extraordinary degree. If we focus on old ways of conducting an audit, we will be unable to audit at the speed of risk and will quickly lose credibility and stature as a trusted resource.

Don't shrink from getting to the bottom of issues. You will always struggle to find the root cause of an issue if you are not open-minded. I have seen internal auditors arrive at the end of the audit process and still display a stunning lack of understanding of the issue. For example, they may report a condition (a failure in a control in a certain area) and an unsupported, under-researched cause (the people in that area are not adequately trained), then provide an underwhelming or painfully obvious recommendation (do a better job training). Well, that may look fine, albeit uninspiring, on the surface. But what if the cause that was articulated wasn't the true root cause of the control failure? Perhaps there was no reinforcement mechanism in place to drive employees to follow company policies. Or maybe culture was the culprit: possibly the prevailing corporate philosophy was one of the ends justifying the means, thereby excusing the lack of effective controls. The point is, if you are complacent and not open to digging deeper, you are unlikely to get to the root cause and, as a consequence, your value will be significantly diminished.

Don't take a myopic view in making recommendations. The easy solution may be right, but it also may not. In many instances, if the obvious solution was the right one, chances are that it would have already been conceived and implemented. It's best to assume there is a reason that solution isn't already in place; maybe it has been tried and abandoned because of a lack of success, or it wasn't assessed as a critical enough risk to even test the solution. Open-mindedness calls for creativity—being willing to explore alternative explanations for why something happened and proposing creative solutions for ensuring it doesn't happen again. Of course, there is some risk to this approach. Lars Christensen reminds us that there are people who will mistake internal audit's guidance or recommendation for creative solutions as "approval by the auditors" to do what they want. This should not cause us to abandon creativity, however; we simply have to be prepared to defend our recommendations with as much creativity as we used to develop them.

Don't neglect to seek input from those you are auditing. Internal auditors are often compared, rarely flatteringly, with police officers. So let's imagine a police officer stops you for speeding and prepares to give you a ticket. You respond by suggesting that the two of you work together to find a different solution, rather than a ticket. While the officer would probably be disinclined to consider such an option, this is metaphorically what internal auditors must sometimes be willing to do in their audits.

One of the AEC survey respondents pointed out how critical this aspect of open-mindedness is to an activity in which internal auditors participate on a regular basis: negotiation. Effective negotiation means not automatically imposing your own solution when another may be just as good or better; it is based on an appreciation for what can be achieved if we are open to alternatives. We must be willing to hear our clients' views, discuss them, and work toward a mutually acceptable solution.

Don't view the world in black and white. There are often multiple paths to the same outcome. Outstanding internal auditors explore these paths, discuss their advantages and disadvantages, and assess their risk. An ability to navigate ambiguity was specifically called out by one of the AEC survey respondents who described it as "comfort and skill in dealing with competing truths." I like that particular definition as it seems especially pertinent to internal auditing. The ability to see beyond black and white ties in with a point I made on ethical resiliency in chapter 2: the need to leave preconceived notions at the door. Never enter an audit with your findings, solutions, or opinion of the involved parties already in mind.

WHO CARES?

You might think I am overemphasizing open-mindedness as a key characteristic of outstanding internal auditors. It may seem softer and more touchy-feely than some of the other traits discussed in this book. But believe me, I see nothing soft, nothing trivial, about this trait. In fact, I credit open-mindedness in part for success in my career.

Throughout my professional life I have strived to be open to new opportunities, new adventures, and new perspectives. Like many others, I have a healthy respect for career opportunities with all their commensurate benefits. But I have always been driven by much more. When I grew weary in a position, I knew I was no longer learning or growing. I refused to be caught in a rut, and even left a higher-paying position simply because it was ceaselessly routine and mundane. I frequently advise young internal auditors to not be afraid to move to another company or leave the profession for a while and return when recharged. Be open to ways that expand your skills.

If you are not finding ways to express your openness in your job, the problem may not be with the job. It may be with you. Perhaps you are not looking hard enough. Early in my career I was part of a team conducting audits in Panama related to the canal treaty implementation. We found that some of the records on costs related to refurbishing the facilities were incomplete. We talked to the engineer responsible for record-keeping and shared with him our preliminary conclusion that the documentation maintained by his staff was "unauditable." He was outraged, a response that left a lasting impression on me. He claimed we were the ones at fault by not recognizing the complexity of the environment and the difficulty of keeping all the records straight.

We seemed to be at a standoff until my colleague who was in charge of the audit calmly and professionally led us to a mutually satisfactory agreement. Instead of using the term "unauditable," we would describe the records as "not readily auditable." A minor distinction, you might say. But I consider it a prime example of being open-minded. The source documents were still in existence, so it was possible to pull together complete material, just with some extra effort. We felt the flexibility in nomenclature was justified for the greater good of getting what we wanted—auditable records. We didn't conceal the problem (we clearly said the records weren't auditable), but our actions allowed the engineer to comply with the objective of assembling complete, auditable records. And that's exactly what happened. We issued a correct report, the engineer's pride and reputation were left intact because he was empowered to fix the problem, and everything turned out fine.

Similarly, Aileen Madden found that taking a different path helped meet objectives. Her company's internal audit function did not have a clear view of the company's business continuity planning process. After considerable digging, the team realized that while there were indeed continuity plans developed for the most critical areas of the business, there was no coordinated effort to ensure they were in place for *all* areas of the business or that they adequately addressed the risk of severe business interruptions. The audit team determined the root cause was a lack of ownership, skills, and resources to do the work.

"We could have audited the area and issued a report with multiple findings (which, with the lack of resources and skills may not have been addressed anyway), but instead, we helped management gain agreement to hire outside assistance to perform a business impact assessment on the most critical areas of the business," Madden says. The objective was twofold: to address the highest-risk areas of the business and develop a standard methodology to enable the business to perform business impact assessments in other areas of the company. This open-mindedness built trust between internal audit and the particular area of the business.

"We demonstrated that we have their best interests in mind," Madden explains. "We are not there to throw them under the bus, but to help them meet their objectives. Had we not been willing to alter our approach to addressing this risk area, we may have alienated the business by issuing a damning audit report, and not have been any closer to mitigating the risk."

Those are two good examples of how open-mindedness can help navigate through the unexpected. But it's a skill that is equally useful—no, critical—even when we know exactly what to expect, which in today's environment can involve complexity, ambiguity, diversity of thought, and a plethora of solutions. If we don't care about surviving in these choppy professional waters, what in the world do we care about?

Despite an array of benefits to being open-minded, some may find it difficult to overcome some intrinsic, deeply engrained human fears: letting go of control, making ourselves vulnerable, making mistakes, and being completely honest with ourselves. That last one—being as open with ourselves as we are with others—may be especially difficult. It certainly requires us to reconsider our assumptions—not an easy task, because assumptions are hard-wired into most of us. They contribute to our ability to navigate safely through the world. If we see someone take a steaming pot of soup off the stove, we assume the burner is hot, so we stay away from it. That's healthy and a necessary assumption to sustain.

But some assumptions are just a lazy way to interpret comments, events, or behaviors. They save us from having to think too hard about new meanings. They also can inhibit our ability to be open-minded. Noted science fiction author Isaac Asimov—a pretty open-minded individual himself—pointed that out when he observed, "Your assumptions are your windows on the world. Scrub them off every once in a while, or the light won't come in."[2] In fact, so effective is open-mindedness in countering an overreliance on assumptions and other lazy mental behaviors that some psychologists term it a "corrective virtue"—it corrects the faults that accompany closed behaviors.

Outstanding internal auditors understand that open-mindedness does not imply indecisiveness or an inability to think for one's self. Instead, it is the willingness, even courage, to search actively for evidence against previously favored beliefs, plans, or goals, then weigh such evidence fairly and objectively. Far from being wishy-washy, open-minded people tend to take a firm stand on a position and act accordingly, precisely because they know they have given the various alternatives full and open consideration.

I opened this chapter with an old joke about internal auditors and lightbulbs. But outstanding internal auditors would likely not be the subject of such a joke. They simply wouldn't be changing the lightbulbs every year. They would have identified the need to install long-life, compact fluorescent lamps years ago, thereby negating the need to change them every year. Or perhaps they would have identified "green solutions" to enhance the natural lighting, eliminating the need for lightbulbs entirely.

As my tongue-in-cheek analogies illustrate, we must always be looking beyond the obvious solutions and be open to change in "the way things are done around here." And we must be willing to share alternative solutions for our client's consideration by leveraging outstanding communication skills, which is the subject of the next chapter.

RELATIONAL ATTRIBUTES

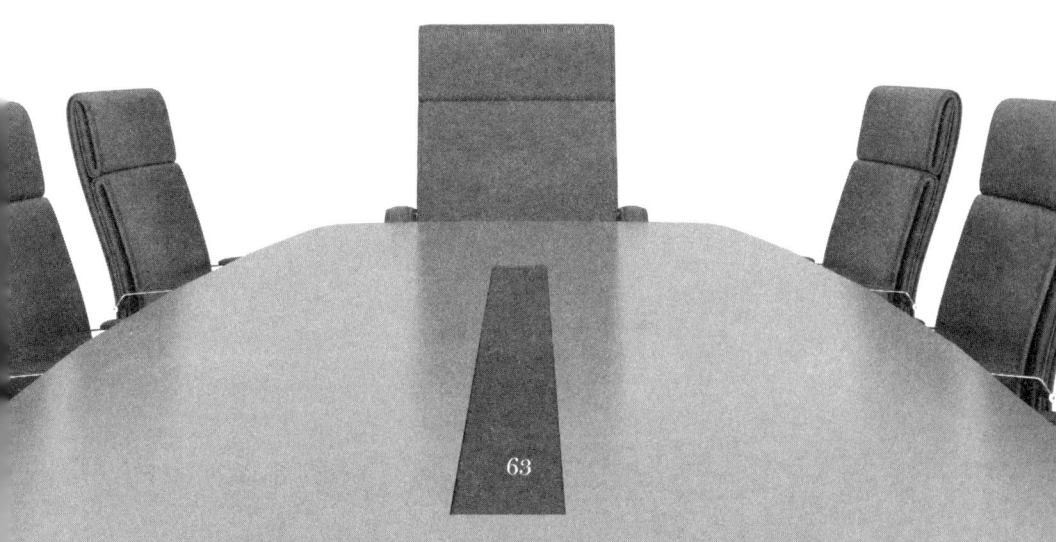

CHAPTER 6

DYNAMIC COMMUNICATORS

AS SOMEONE WHO has evangelized the importance of communication skills in internal auditing for many years, I observed early in my career that internal auditors who were eloquent in conversation and on paper were far more effective at achieving results and winning the respect and trust of those they audit. Yet, I also observed that such individuals were few and far between. The fact was that the vast majority in our profession were introverts—much happier to pour over a good set of workpapers than to engage the organization's management in a hallway conversation. The old joke that "an extroverted auditor is someone who looks at *your* shoes when talking with you" hit just a little too close to home for many of us in the profession.

Introverts may have been effective in an era where we were "counting the beans." However, with the advent of operational auditing in the late twentieth century, we had to be able to do more than communicate numbers. It became essential that we be conversant on the risks and controls that confront the business, and for many internal auditors, that was a game changer. Today, communication skills are table stakes (alongside integrity) in the minds of many CAEs. If you are not a strong communicator, then there is no place for you in many of the world's leading internal audit staffs. An outstanding internal auditor with extraordinary communication skills is often seen as a crown jewel in any internal audit department.

Most people would ascribe a plethora of traits in order to render communication effective. In essence, however, communication should be concise, clear, conversational, and complete. It should take into account the priorities and expectations of the audience, make use of effective questioning, be built on body language and eye contact, start with the headline and fill in the details later, and focus on the positive.

I certainly can't argue with any of those characteristics. In *Lessons Learned on the Audit Trail*, I included my own list of effective communication techniques customized for internal auditing.

But where many definitions and lists fall short is in identifying the overarching goal of communication. Those who craft such lists do a great job explaining *how* to communicate better but fail to articulate *why* strong communication skills are so critical to an internal auditor's success. To that end, I find guidance provided by Dr. John Lund, a retired adjunct professor who taught at universities throughout Washington, Idaho, California, and Utah and a consultant who specializes in interpersonal communications, to be particularly useful. "Don't communicate to be understood," he counsels. "Rather, communicate so as not to be misunderstood."[1] I like that advice because it ties together all the techniques of good communication but places the emphasis where I think it belongs: on the audience.

Our primary purpose in communicating should not be to say our piece. That implies we are the center of focus and our communication should suit our own purposes. Instead, we should communicate to ensure there is a clear understanding on the part of the listeners (or readers). That places the spotlight directly on them. Our speech or document should emphasize what we believe to be of interest or benefit to them. It doesn't mean we don't make our point, but we do it in a way that puts them first.

COMMUNICATION AND INTERNAL AUDITORS

Many people might doubt that internal auditors are an ideal study group on effective communication. Indeed, the results of the widely followed Myers-Briggs personality assessment typically place accountants and auditors squarely in the introvert category. However, the CAEs who responded to the AEC survey on outstanding internal auditor traits had no doubt about the importance of effective communication. It was the highest-rated trait, with nearly 6 out of 10 respondents ranking it among their top three attributes. Absolutely no one—literally, 0 percent—left it off their top 10 list. The CBOK 2015 Practitioner Survey indicated that communication was one of the top two most sought after skills by CAEs recruiting candidates.[2]

George Aubrey, vice president and chief auditor of Lenovo Group, sums up the prevailing view: "You can be the best technical auditor ever created when it comes to determining precisely what is at risk, identifying related key controls, designing the best tests, and drawing the right conclusions. But if you're unable to communicate to stakeholders in a way that drives change, you're like the proverbial tree that falls in the forest—no one hears."

Russ Charlton, senior vice president and chief auditor at Time Inc., sees the importance of strong communication similarly: "That is our deliverable. No one sees all the work that goes on behind the scenes. What our clients see and hear is what we communicate to them. It's how they judge us and our work." The consensus is clear. Those who reach the pinnacle of the internal audit profession know that you can't get there without a mastery of communication.

THE SOFTER SIDE

The findings of the AEC survey aren't shocking. Communication ranks high on every survey of internal audit skills I've seen in recent years. But I was a bit surprised at how several AEC survey respondents described the aspect of communication they find most critical to success in internal auditing. It's not the technical side of communication (being succinct, clear, correct, etc.); it's the "soft" side, which they describe as emotional intelligence.

They refer to the importance of nonverbal cues—reading between the lines of facial expressions and body gestures—and selecting the appropriate response based on these perceptions. They embrace the notion that this sort of communication can be built only on a firm foundation of self-awareness—knowing our personal biases and tendencies, recognizing how others view us, and understanding how to use our emotions constructively. I have participated in many meetings between internal auditors and their clients where, if relying on a transcript of what was said was the only form of communication, it would have been completely misleading in assessing the effectiveness of the meeting. On the other hand, a video of the meeting—even without sound—would have been incredibly revealing about the communication between the parties. As a former CAE, I frequently coached my staff to be mindful of their body language and observe that of audit clients during meetings, and then adjust the delivery of their message accordingly.

They are also keenly aware of the deceptively challenging issue of behaving in a personable and approachable manner. I think this is especially critical for those internal auditors who aspire to be trusted advisors. In my view, trusted advisors are approachable. But, more than that, they also do the approaching. If we proclaim to be trusted advisors but just sit at our desks waiting for others to come to us for advice, we will likely be pretty lonely. Conversely, if we go out and cultivate relationships through ongoing communication, people will ultimately seek us out—an outcome that holds true for all the different hats we wear as internal auditors, whether as assurance providers or advisors.

We cannot build relationships without effective use of communication. Dan VanSciver, CAE of Sallie Mae, is one of the many who consider effective communication the top attribute needed by internal auditors, precisely because of its use in forming relationships. "The best auditors on my team are those who build a relationship with the people we audit—not just when we audit them, but throughout the year," he says. "Good communication leads to good relationships, which contribute significantly to good audits."

I agree, but feel compelled to point out the flip side of that scenario. Audits can run into trouble when clients have no relationship with the internal auditors beyond the ongoing engagement. From my experience, the absence of any relationship prior to a particularly contentious audit can be a prescription for disaster in terms of the audit's outcome. If there is no basis for trust, or management has doubts about the credibility of the audit team, they will often either ignore or push back on critical findings and recommendations.

SETTING THE RIGHT TONE

It's one thing to agree that internal auditors need communication skills, but one skill I believe is paramount to internal auditors mastering communication is tone. We are much more likely to achieve success in facilitating change if we avoid appearing accusatory or threatening in our communications.

I recall an instance early in my career when someone read a draft of my audit report and said, "I agree with the recommendations, but I disagree with all of the findings." In other words, the individual didn't take exception with the fact that I had found issues that needed to be addressed; he wasn't even reluctant to fix the problems. What he resisted was the *tone* of my report. Its critical nature caused him to push back hard. It was a valuable lesson. If our tone is one of pointing fingers or speaking down, we will dig ourselves into a deep hole that will be hard to climb out of—especially the next time we interact with that person. We must strive to maintain open, civil, and productive communication at all times.

As a senior auditor many years ago, I was teamed with another internal auditor. We went into an entrance briefing and my colleague immediately began talking about why we were there. The first words out of my colleague's mouth were, "Your area is being audited because it was rated as a high-risk area in our annual risk assessment." No small talk, no warmup—just straight to business. That is not wrong in itself. What was ill-advised was the way this person approached the subject by launching into how the risk assessment had identified the area as high-risk and susceptible to poor controls, and that other officials in the organization let us know we would likely find a lot of issues. Technically, my colleague was correct—even truthful—but the person's approach could not have been more wrong. I quickly saw hackles going up around the room, so I stepped in to calm things down. It was not a matter of being particularly adept, I had just put myself in their shoes and imagined how I would feel upon hearing this message. The information was accurate, but the tone of the delivery was faulty, because the person hadn't mastered the skill that outstanding internal auditors develop over time—sensing what tone is appropriate to elicit the desired response.

Internal auditors have a special challenge with tone because so much of what we do is through written communication. When the medium is just words on a page or screen, it's difficult to convey empathy and warmth, and nearly impossible to gauge the reaction of the audience. Audit reports are not known for being comforting. We have to remember that those reading the reports often view them through two lenses, neither of which is conducive to joy. They see the reports as an attack on their competency or even integrity, or they worry how their boss or the board will perceive them after reading the report. Both concerns are justifiable, but they can be ameliorated by tone and a judicious use of a technique internal auditors fail to use as often as they should: recognition of achievements. "Never hang a client out to dry," says Michael Rimkus, vice president of internal audit and risk management and CAE of T-Mobile U.S. Inc. Everyone appreciates a pat on the back from time to time.

FIVE WORDS OR PHRASES TO AVOID

Recognizing the challenges internal auditors face in communicating effectively in writing, I blogged some time ago on the five words or phrases that should be eliminated from internal audit reports. Not that they are necessarily wrong, but I believe they are ineffective because they assign blame, are imprecise, could be construed as a personal attack, or position the internal auditor inappropriately. That list included "failed," "inadequate," "ineffective," "we found," and "it appears." I suspect that you can come up with many others, but I think the point is made. Tone matters and it is harder to convey in written form, so weigh your words carefully.

As a former CAE, I insisted that internal audit reports issued by my departments include a "management accomplishments" section that would appear early in the report. In this section, we would note our observations of areas that were well controlled or well managed. We would highlight any improvements that had been made since the last audit and any leading practices we observed during the audit. This wasn't simply pandering to the client. I believed that it conveyed our objectivity and created a more balanced report. Clients were typically very receptive to this section of the report, and it sometimes helped ameliorate their frustrations with the often critical findings and conclusions that would follow.

Using language the reader understands is also critical. George Aubrey says that when issues become sensitive enough to be escalated to him, he finds himself scratching his head. The facts in the case seem clear and unequivocal. But quite often, the underlying issue is one of communication. "It's not uncommon that the auditor has failed to translate the message from audit-speak to the language of the business," Aubrey notes. "It seems like a relatively insignificant thing, but this failure to communicate can cause inefficiencies in the company and negatively affect the internal audit brand."

But tone is not just the words selected; it is also respect for the reader's time. Give busy readers a break and let them assimilate the message quickly. The sooner they grasp key points the more likely they are to read to the end. A phrase that is used in many contexts is especially fitting in internal auditing: be brief and be gone.

WHAT ELSE?

Communication is not only about effectively speaking out; attentive listening is equally important. It seems like it should be so easy, but listening—focused listening—can be more difficult than talking, especially for extroverts. The late Bernard Baruch, an American financier and advisor to presidents, said a characteristic of many of the successful people he knew was to do more listening than talking.[3] Yet the vast majority of people are probably more like those described by the late Stephen Covey, author of *The 7 Habits of Highly Effective People: Powerful Lessons in Personal Change*: they listen not with the intent to understand but with the intent to reply.[4] Attentive listening calls for us to focus solely on the person speaking. We must put down our devices, shut down our laptops, establish eye contact, and make every effort to glean information from what the individual says—and what they don't say. It is easier said than done.

Michael Rimkus brings the point home to internal auditing. He says, "We take a no-surprises approach. We believe that, if we listen attentively to what our audit clients say and then communicate effectively and consistently throughout the audit process, making sure to portray the client's perspective in our reporting, there should be no surprises. Good communication means satisfied clients." Outstanding internal auditors excel at listening to others. That's how they learn, how they build relationships, and how they demonstrate and, consequently, earn trust.

KEEP IT SIMPLE

The ability to take something complex and simplify it is another key element of communication, and one with which many internal auditors struggle. Some feel compelled to share with their audiences every bit of information discovered, every test conducted, and every bit of data analyzed. Perhaps they think it is impressive. In reality, it is more likely frustrating and/or sleep-inducing. "Audit findings can be complex and/or detailed. An effective communicator finds ways to synthesize the information and make it easy to understand," points out Richard Brilliant, chief audit officer of Carnival Corp. & PLC. "This may require creating charts, graphs, or infographics. But all too often, I see auditors who take the easy way out and rely on a data dump when communicating. This approach is ineffective time and time again." Of course, it requires time and thought to distill a mass of information to a few salient, relevant points that will be of benefit to the client. But it's worth the effort. The old sayings "keep it simple" and "less is more" exist for a reason.

Another important communication skill involves the art of persuasion. Results are not achieved until management implements internal audit's recommendations and they produce a desired outcome. Often, inspiring that reaction in management calls for persuasion. Persuasion doesn't rely on flashy eloquence, an arcane vocabulary, or a dramatic presentation. It's actually fairly simple: phrase your recommendations in ways that incentivize listeners to embrace them, because doing so will make them more successful.

It's not just a matter of phrasing, though. There must be sincerity behind it. You must truly want to help and be honestly interested in making the audited area or the company better. I have found that a good approach is to position your messages as often as possible in terms of risk. For example, let's say the audit reveals an outdated policy on how to evaluate potential contractors—a policy that doesn't take into account recent advances in technology. Internal auditors must convey the risks that could arise if the policy isn't updated. For example, if contractors are not thoroughly evaluated, there is an increased risk that those selected may be unable to meet the contract requirements, causing the organization to suffer inefficiencies or lost resources. The focus on risk eliminates finger wagging and, instead, directs attention to how mitigating the risk will make the area more effective and efficient, potentially driving shareholder value. Good managers will almost always respond to the opportunity to improve their area and their company, and their self-preservation instincts alone will cause their ears to perk up when risk is being discussed.

A focus on risk doesn't apply solely to clients. It should be a key element when speaking with senior management and the audit committee as well. Russ Charlton reminds us that discussions about risk require special care. "You can usually talk to the audit committee about external risks to the company all day long without offending anyone. But when you start talking about internal risks—maybe changes are needed in management or culture is getting in the way of the enterprise's success—that's when it can become sensitive. Effective communication enables you to let the audit committee know that a real risk exists without throwing anyone under the bus. It's threading a pretty fine needle sometimes."

I've mentioned in several contexts the need to put ourselves in others' shoes. Dr. Lund believes that most people in a business setting want to know three things before they are willing to enter into a conversation:

1. Is what you want to talk about going to be painful?

2. How long is it going to take?

3. When you are through talking, what will you want from me?[5]

If you find that people avoid your meetings or fail to return your phone calls, it may be that they don't have good answers to those three questions. All three are extremely pertinent to internal auditors, especially when it's nearly time to deliver the final report and recommendations. Clients are often concerned that the result of the audit will be painful. Address this concern by keeping them informed along the way so there are no surprises, shocking or otherwise. They want to know how much more of their time is needed, given that they probably feel they have already surrendered quite a bit just going through the audit. Be respectful of their time throughout the engagement and stick to the agreed-upon duration. And, of course, they'll want to know what they need to do to comply with the recommendations in the audit report. Again, the no-surprises approach is helpful here, as are the persuasion skills discussed earlier. If you focus on risk and its potential impact on the organization, the client is more likely to consider the follow-up actions as benefiting the organization, not just "doing what the auditors told us we had to do."

STORM CLOUDS ON THE HORIZON

About a month after the AEC survey was conducted, the results from the annual North American Pulse of Internal Audit survey[6] came in. Completed by almost 500 CAEs and directors/senior managers, survey respondents singled out communication for its criticality to internal audit: 98 percent of the respondents indicate it is very or extremely essential to their internal audit function's ability to perform its responsibilities. Despite that ringing commendation of the importance of communication, these CAEs aren't particularly positive about their staff's relevant capabilities. Only 55 percent consider their team very or extremely proficient in listening actively, and an even smaller proportion (41 percent) characterize their team as very or extremely proficient in organizing and expressing ideas clearly.

Contrast that with the findings from the CBOK survey,[7] which highlighted that "a strong majority of board members [gave] high scores for the quality (83 percent) and the frequency (81 percent) of internal audit's communications with them." What does this say? For stakeholders, effective communication is a key imperative to enable the audit committee to work with internal audit in addressing any gaps in the annual audit plan. They trust internal audit to communicate effectively and provide them with a seat at the table. In the Pulse survey, 14 percent of the CAEs rely on recruiting for those skills (active listening and clear expression); the remaining 86 percent train for them.

While the recruitment percentage may be low because of the perception that it is easier to train those skills and instead recruit for technical skills, it's possible that it's also difficult to find people already so equipped. That's the issue facing Richard Brilliant, who notes, "I find it harder to locate talent that has high competency with communication skills. Finding talent with audit/technical skills is easier by comparison." But he is well aware of the problem that imbalance raises, saying, "It doesn't matter how good your technical skills are if you are unable to effectively communicate and persuade."

Internal Auditor magazine ran an article on teaching internal auditing to university students. The article[8] reflects the views of professors, recent students, and job recruiters who unanimously agree on the importance and value of teaching soft skills as part of the curriculum. Unfortunately, the time available in the typical class period simply does not allow professors to address both the soft and the technical skills required in the profession. One professor points out that his time with his students in a typical semester is about 40 hours—the equivalent of one workweek. Clearly, a problem exists for which there is no easy answer, but an answer needs to be found.

By near-unanimous agreement, communication is essential to successful internal auditing. However, the talent pool is small and the approaches for growing it are limited. This is not a minor issue or a problem that can be set aside until it is more convenient; the future effectiveness of internal audit is at stake. If communication cannot be taught in the formal university environment, we need to find other ways to encourage its development. Certainly, formal corporate training programs are one method—and an effective one. But I also believe the trusted advisors in our profession should play a role by mentoring others in their organizations who struggle with communication. In demonstrating their extraordinary communication skills to their peers, they also help them to appreciate how relationship acumen can be integral to success.

CHAPTER 7

INSIGHTFUL RELATIONSHIPS

OVER THE COURSE of my career, the most enduring lessons learned were rooted in my first job as an internal auditor. One of those valuable lessons was the importance of insightful relationships. As an Army civilian audit trainee, my training plan for the first two years mandated that I spend rotational assignments in each of the other controller functions (where internal audit reported at the time). I spent six weeks working side by side with colleagues in the budget, accounting, program management, and cost analysis departments. While the rotational assignments were primarily designed for me to learn about the missions and objectives of each of these departments, it was the relationships that I developed with management and staff that would prove to be the most enduring benefit.

Once these rotational assignments were completed, I found myself assigned to audit teams that would invariably return to these departments during the course of audit assignments. However, instead of a nameless audit trainee who showed up to ask questions or peruse their records, management and staff in these departments saw me as a colleague—someone they had come to know during the time I had spent with them during the rotational assignments. And I saw them as colleagues who had helped me to understand their world—not under the glare of an ongoing audit but as a peer who was there to learn from them. In many ways I had a natural advantage over my internal audit colleagues who had not experienced the rotational assignment model. I had the benefit of entering each engagement with strong relationships that gave me insight into understanding them, which made the audit process and outcome much better.

One of the most important lessons I have learned about relationships is that the way we treat others often determines how they treat us. Like many internal auditors, I have worked with colleagues who apparently were born skeptics, always presuming those they audit have done something wrong or have something to hide. Their mission is often to uncover misdeeds and bring down the offending parties. It's not difficult to envision where this attitude typically leads. It's not difficult to envision that this attitude typically leads to poor performance, and work relationships suffer for it. A gradual breakdown in communication with management—often with the CAEs who lead their departments—may lead clients to withhold information during risk assessments and audit engagements. information during risk assessments and audit engagements. Their negative behaviors doom their fates as trusted advisors.

While I am sure most people reading this book have worked with naysayers, we have all worked with people who are polar opposites— those whose skills in developing, building, and sustaining relationships contribute directly to their success. There is a direct correlation between character and fate. In the work environment, character often manifests in the quality and quantity of relationships.

NOT JUST A POPULARITY CONTEST

We all know people who seem to make friends effortlessly. They attract others like a magnet; like bees drawn to honey. These people are not in the majority. Most of us have to work hard to build and establish relationships. It takes time, effort, and perseverance. But given all we have to do just to get our jobs done every day, who has time for this? And is it even necessary?

You know the answer to that. Yes. Absolutely. No question. Good relationships do not just make everyone feel better; they are integral to success within the internal audit function and, more importantly, to becoming a trusted advisor. In *Lessons Learned on the Audit Trail*, I described two elements as necessary to becoming a trusted advisor. One was relationship acumen. My opinion of its importance hasn't changed;

if anything, my appreciation of its benefits has increased. In deciding on the title of this chapter, I wrestled a bit with how to describe this characteristic of outstanding internal auditors better than "relationship acumen." When I think of relationship acumen in terms of a trait, it's more about intuition and having the insight into building relationships.

Kevin Patton, director of internal audit for The Ohio State University, is a staunch supporter of relationship building, emphasizing its importance in the higher education environment. "In corporations, the decision-making process is very top-down. The CEO makes a decision, and it is disseminated down through the ranks. In higher education, we have a shared governance model. Faculty, administrators, even students have a say in how the university operates. So working together through relationships is paramount." Corporate executives who are brought into a university setting, Patton explains, often have trouble making the transition to this shared governance approach. "Shared governance depends on relationships—and, yes, building those relationships can slow down the process, but it is critical to getting needed buy-in."

RELATIONSHIP BUILDING STARTS AT "HOME"

Before trusted advisors can build strong and effective relationships with clients, they must cultivate strong relationships with their peers and those for whom they work, such as the CAE. People who are good at building and maintaining relationships tend to have a high degree of social skill, sometimes referred to as social intelligence. Social intelligence supports team building by helping to predict how people will work together. It also provides insight beyond what may initially appear to be a team's task-related difficulties, so that underlying interpersonal problems can be diagnosed and managed.[1]

For internal auditors, skills that bolster teamwork are critical because audit engagements are often undertaken as a team. And without cohesiveness, an individual's personality or agenda may undermine the process. I recall an instance when an insecure team member was so afraid of not getting credit for unearthing information during the audit that workpapers were hidden until they could be presented directly to the boss. Apart from being stunned by the behavior, seldom have I seen such a blatant lack of appreciation for the value of healthy relationships.

I witnessed the importance of relationships and team chemistry repeatedly as we were building the inspector general's office in the U.S. Postal Service. As I noted earlier, we hired hundreds of auditors from government and industry in a short period of time. Virtually every week we were initiating new audits led by teams of individuals who had never worked together before. The results were often frustrating at the time and fascinating in retrospect.

Some teams came together and worked very well devising and executing an audit plan. Those teams were often comprised of individuals who were results oriented and possessed a higher degree of relationship-building skills. However, some teams struggled because of one or two individuals whose personalities were fraught with challenges and did not work well with others. Their audits took longer to complete and often added less value. Finally, on some occasions, multiple members of the team were conflict prone, and the absence of relationship insight on the team was extremely damaging. In those instances, audits took an incredibly long time, as well as a great deal of my time as deputy inspector general and the time of other managers. I often found myself mediating disputes between two or more team members whose temperament made it difficult for nearly anything to get done.

One of the most critical relationships an internal auditor will have is with his or her CAE. After all, it will be almost impossible to become a trusted advisor with clients and management within the organization if there is no trust between you and your boss. But what happens when a CAE decides that an otherwise talented internal auditor just doesn't fit into his or her organization? Or when the relationship gets so bad that the CAE won't even speak to the staff auditor? While less common in the corporate sector where it is easier to reassign or sever employment relationships, I have witnessed this scenario many times in government internal audit functions where employment relationships are more prescriptive.

As I observed in a blog I wrote several years ago, broken relationships between CAEs and members of their team can be repaired.[2] For a CAE who finds himself or herself in a broken relationship with a team member, I suggested five steps to "rehabilitating" the relationship and returning that person to the productive fold:

1. Sit down and objectively chronicle the issues or events that caused the loss of confidence in your audit subordinate. (You may even find that you cannot remember the triggering event or events.)

2. Take the time to document the individual's strengths and weaknesses. The weaknesses will often be obvious if there is a legitimate basis for loss of trust.

3. Forge a plan to communicate honestly and openly about the state of the relationship. Ask the organization's human resources professional for assistance or advice.

4. Establish a plan to repair and rehabilitate the relationship. Specific goals and agreed-upon measures should be set, but keep in mind there should be flexibility in the specific solutions proposed.

5. Communication should take place regularly and openly throughout the recovery process. If the relationship has any chance of recovery, communication will be a key factor.

For the internal auditor whose relationship with the CAE is broken, I offered this advice:

1. Signal your interest in resetting the relationship. If the CAE doesn't take the lead, propose at least five steps as a path to recovery.

2. Never forget that the CAE is the boss. You may not like the person, but you won't be effective until you resolve to take direction and adapt to the way the CAE wants to run the internal audit function.

3. Take a critical look at yourself. These scenarios are rarely one-sided. Are you a hard worker? Are you poised, polished, and professional? Do you exemplify the values of the organization? If you solicit the CAE's

candid assessment, you are apt to hear things that will force you to take a close look at yourself.

4. Commit to "getting out of the dog house." It will take hard work and determination to constantly exceed the likely low expectations of your skeptical CAE.

5. If you believe the root cause of the problem is an absolute lack of respect or trust for your CAE, then resolve to leave the organization. Life is too short to work under such circumstances.

STRONG RELATIONSHIPS WITH CLIENTS: THE ULTIMATE OBJECTIVE

While strong relationships within the team are essential to the overall success of the organization, it is the strong relationships with clients and other stakeholders where outstanding trusted advisors differentiate themselves. After all, most of us would rather do business with a person or a company we know. We are confident they will do a good job, and we count on them to be courteous and fair. And we are more likely to forgive a mistake, because we know they are giving it their best and we fully expect the issue to be resolved to our satisfaction. Such loyalty and trust doesn't happen at first. It develops over time as a relationship is established.

Well-developed relationships can help to overcome negative perceptions and even apprehension about working with internal auditors. Davis Moraes, head of internal audit at Iochpe-Maxion S/A Group, learned an important lesson from a former boss. "He explained that auditors used to be regarded like the police and were generally unwelcome," Moraes says. "So one way to change this paradigm is to be friendly and put ourselves in others' shoes. This makes our clients more receptive and collaborative and the outcome of our work is more valuable." By establishing relationships with our internal clients and with third parties, we can change negative perceptions and become the "face" of the function. Through the relationships we build, we can foster an understanding of the value of internal audit and defuse a bit of the trepidation some may feel about it.

Another good reason to build strong relationships is the natural inclination for people to talk. They'll talk about their experiences with poor service or a shoddy product they received from an organization, and they'll talk about the places where they were treated like VIPs. The relationships we build help us create great word of mouth for our department, our company, and ourselves (provided we deliver superior performance). There is a reason more and more companies are seeking ways to leverage viral marketing of their products, as opposed to the traditional approach of paid advertising. Research shows that people tend to rely more readily on the opinions of friends or influencers. They believe that what they hear from people like them or people they aspire to be is more likely to be true, tested, and pertinent. If we can get people talking about the good experience they have had with internal audit, we'll make things easier for ourselves in the future.

I am not alone in believing that a focus on relationships is crucial. One of the AEC survey respondents noted, "Adeptly managing client relationships is key, in my opinion, to making the audit function effective. The one thing that I almost always have to fix when I come in as a new CAE is a string of broken relationships." Another pointed out, "Some of the most effective auditors I have seen have been excellent partners with those in other parts of the organizations they serve. They collaborate on discovered issues and problems with others outside of internal audit, without compromising independence or ethics. It is the exact opposite of the 'gotcha' mentality."

YES, BUT HOW?

Understanding the benefits of good relationships is easy, but knowing how to develop them may not be so readily apparent for many of us. Unfortunately, there is no proven recipe for it. In many cases, we have to be sensitive to the situation, the individual(s) involved, and the perceptions of others and determine the best approach on the spot.

Some AEC survey respondents suggested that relationship building should encompass talent development, collaboration, navigation of corporate politics, and coaching. There also are some commonsense techniques. Generally speaking, I find a straightforward, open, and honest approach to be productive. When I performed an audit, I tried to start by getting to know the client(s), if we didn't already have a relationship, and engaging with them in an approachable way. I wanted to understand their perspective and issues and help them understand the role I would play in our upcoming collaboration. I expressed genuine interest in their needs and sincere empathy for any concerns they had, including possible anxiety about the audit itself.

A few years back, I partnered with the Korn/Ferry Institute to examine personal attributes that maximize the impact of CAEs. Relationship acumen was one of the areas we studied in depth. From my experience, when it comes to relationship-building skills, trusted advisors typically demonstrate all six characteristics defined in that report. Allow me to provide you with a synopsis of how these characteristics reinforce relationship skills.

1. **Positive intent.** It is critical for the client to see the internal auditor as fair, independent, and objective in his or her approach and as someone who has everyone's best interests at heart. Trusted advisors demonstrate a positive intent that makes it clear that he or she isn't set on being right, but is set on finding the right answer.

2. **Diplomacy.** Trusted advisors are adept in direct, forthright communication (including listening) skills, political astuteness, and sensitivity to the organization's culture and how things get done. They are intuitive about people and have the ability to read an audience. They are masters at being contrarian without being confrontational.

3. **Prescience.** Identifying the risks ahead requires curiosity, an ability to see matters with fresh eyes, and a willingness to question assumptions. Trusted advisors can "see around corners." They anticipate the needs of clients before the needs are even evident, and they identify issues before they arise.

4. **Trustworthiness.** Trusted advisors walk the talk, keep confidences, operate with integrity, and are obsessive

about maintaining credibility with clients. They are seen as professionals who can be counted on to repeatedly take the same course of action given the same set of circumstances time after time.

5. **Leadership**. Trusted advisors often set the tone for the entire internal audit staff. They are gifted at steering others toward consensus, managing conflict, and gaining alignment on issues.

6. **Empathy**. Trusted advisors understand and focus on each stakeholder's point of view, and they are sensitive to those needs and feelings. He or she must listen. A genuine caring about others amplifies all the other qualities on this list.[3]

These are worthy characteristics to emulate, but let's break it down further. Building good relationships starts very simply: others must find you approachable. This is not just luck of the draw. You can make yourself more approachable by being friendly, open, honest, and helpful. But being approachable is not enough. There also must be professional respect. You must be regarded as competent, the best at what you do. You must be reliable, following up on projects as agreed. And you must behave admirably and treat others with the same respect you hope to gain from them.

In fact, the whole concept of mirroring desired behaviors—treating others as you wish to be treated—is the foundation of all relationship-building efforts. It's the golden rule: "do unto others as you would have them do unto you." If you demonstrate that you value others and can be trusted, if you are proactively helpful, and if you admit when you have made an error and follow it up promptly with efforts to resolve the issue, you should have no trouble building strong and productive business relationships.

Note that I wrote you *should*—not *will*—have no trouble. There is no magic formula that will guarantee success in forging relationships. Sometimes you can try every technique in the book and still get nowhere with the person you are trying to cultivate. As deputy inspector general at the Postal Service, I experienced challenges with several executives in management. It was a challenging dynamic and there were times when we butted heads. In retrospect, I recognize that our difficulty in establishing and cultivating a relationship limited our success. I also acknowledge that there were times I could have done a better job walking the talk as I'm sharing with you today. But, ultimately, relationship building is a two-way street, because it takes communication. There is only so much progress that can be made if the other individual isn't equally invested in making it work. It's hard to build rapport with a lamppost.

FORMING A TEAM

The techniques that apply to building relationships with individuals outside the internal audit function apply within as well. But internal audit is a team sport, so there are some additional wrinkles that arise when getting multiple people in line and moving in the same direction. Outstanding internal auditors recognize this and know to focus much of their effort on creating an effective, efficient, and cohesive team to ensure optimal performance. Without consensus—without speaking as one, for example—the client may push back on the team's recommendations. "After all," they will say, "even the internal auditors don't agree on this." By the way, cohesion on the team does not mean groupthink. By all means, openness and honesty should rule the day when the team is questioning causes or debating recommendations, but this needs to take place *before* sitting down with the client.

Of course, achieving cohesion is not always easy. During my time at PwC, I worked with a number of young and ambitious internal auditors and sometimes learned of disharmony or personality clashes within one of my highly talented engagement teams. I could have waited to see how those tiffs played out, but armed with lessons I learned at the Postal Service years earlier, I chose instead to be proactive and address them early on—hopefully before they negatively affected the quality of our work and our relationship with the client. I didn't always call the team together or tell them I heard trouble was brewing. Rather, I talked to them individually and asked how each thought the engagement was going. If I knew where the friction was occurring, I might take it a step further with the responsible individuals and ask, "How are you getting along with...?" Then I would sit quietly, listen, and watch the body language. It usually didn't take long to get to the root of the problem. I would then explain that success of the engagement depended on them working well together. I would remind them of the importance of the engagement and, if necessary, point out that they would be evaluated on how well they demonstrated teamwork. If none of that worked, I would collaborate with the firm's partners to transfer individuals between teams. Naturally, if problems persisted within the new teams, the individual's performance evaluation would ultimately reflect that.

Positive reinforcement is effective, including within teams. Public recognition always counts more than a private commendation, and the kudos are more valued when they are specific to a behavior. In other words, congratulating someone on being a team player is not nearly as effective as telling him what a great job he did working with others to pull together the audit report on a tight deadline. One caveat: be sensitive to the overuse of positive reinforcement. Anything, including a compliment, loses meaning when it is repeated too frequently.

Positive reinforcement can also be used effectively even when the core message is not so positive. Leading with a pat on the back makes the rest of the message easier to assimilate, as in, "Your presentation covered all the important points we needed to get across and you handled the follow-up questions very well. But next time, keep an eye on the clock so we don't run over the time allotment we agreed for the meeting." The important thing to remember in a team environment is to avoid favoritism. Treating one person like a superstar is likely to cause the others to become discouraged, and productivity will suffer.

Speaking of superstars, I mentioned earlier that some of the AEC survey respondents cited talent development as a key element of building relationships. It is indeed a skill that should be on the agenda for every CAE and trusted advisor. I especially like the fact that the survey respondents referred to it as developing talent as opposed to developing leaders. When I see someone on my team who has future leadership skills, I am careful to not focus exclusively on that person. I'll naturally help and provide pertinent guidance and suggestions, but I will also spend ample time with those who do not show those skills. My experience is that those who have that leadership drive will get there without a lot of hand-holding. It's the ones who are reluctant, who lack self-confidence, or who don't have relationship acumen who offer CAEs the biggest return in terms of time. Bringing them along allows you to create a team that consists of many strong players. It builds bench strength. If you focus on just the promising individuals, you'll end up with a couple of marquis players and a whole lot of second-stringers. Which team do you think will be more effective?

LONG-TERM CARE

Trusted advisors understand that, even in the best of circumstances, the process of building and sustaining relationships is a never-ending task. Senior executives come and go or change hats, and the audit committee roster changes. You must reach out early and often when personnel change. Tending to long-standing relationships is also imperative. Picking up the phone or extending a lunch invitation to talk through a touchy issue pays enormous dividends to the trusted advisor and the entire internal audit staff.

Building trust and understanding in others requires an investment of time and energy, in part because the needs and expectations of internal audit's stakeholders are constantly evolving. Trusted advisors recognize the signs of change and recalibrate as needed. In the long run, success depends on a balanced mix of relationship building and the ability to identify risks—and then using the results as a basis for creating value.

TAKING THE RISK

There is no denying that developing good working relationships offers a lot of benefits. Of course, with those benefits come risks, and relationship building is no different. Internal auditors are accustomed to thinking about risk and its ramifications, and we are well aware that effective risk management is key to a company's success. However, we may not think of risk in terms of relationships. Yet, the breakdown of a relationship can have a significant impact on our own success or the success of our company. It can take years to build a good relationship and minutes to destroy it. Part of the relationship-building process should involve a prudent consideration of risk, including the possible need for an exit strategy. Granted, most business relationships do not carry this much baggage, but trusted advisors recognize the importance of anticipating a wide range of potential outcomes.

The most significant risk that trusted advisors must take into account relative to relationships is the perception of others. Finding that balance between enjoying healthy, productive work relationships and ensuring that nothing we do could cause others to wonder if our relationships compromise our impartiality is key. There are two dimensions of independence: objectivity of fact and objectivity of appearance.

There is some gray area in how far to take a relationship. "Relationship building is a great tool when it is done with respect and professionalism," Moraes confirms, "but when it goes to an extreme, it can backfire. CAEs must demonstrate maturity and discernment in their relationships within the company." The onus is upon us to ensure we are not negligent in how we manage our interactions with others. We have to view ourselves through the eyes of a third party. Are we doing anything to cause a reasonable person to think we are no longer objective?

Granted, some people will believe what they want to believe regardless of the evidence. We can't allow that to influence our work. Most importantly, we cannot take the route of avoiding improper perceptions of our relationships by having none at all. That is counterproductive in a business context and harmful to us as human beings. We are, by nature, social creatures—even at the office.

The sustainability of any relationship over time is predicated on building and sustaining trust. I firmly believe that trust comes through relationships formed around honesty, empathy, and sincerity. Of course, this doesn't occur without effort. Priorities may need to be adjusted to give relationship building appropriate and consistent emphasis that includes time, effort, and dedication. Those who build and sustain strong relationships are not only successful in achieving their own goals, they also serve as an inspiration to others.

CHAPTER 8

INSPIRATIONAL LEADERS

I HAVE BEEN fortunate to work for a number of inspiring leaders during my career. General Colin Powell, one of my first bosses when I became a CAE, was extremely supportive of me and the internal audit function I led. He displayed genuine interest in my career and inspired me to pursue a career-altering strategic studies program at the U.S. Army War College. Ernie Gregory, my first boss at the Pentagon, was an incredible orator who inspired me to enhance my own leadership and speaking skills as I guided the Army's internal review community through the most tumultuous period in its history. Bill Bishop, The IIA's president from 1992 to 2004, inspired me to alter my post-government career plans and join him in a leadership role at The IIA's headquarters. Each of these towering figures was a gifted and inspirational leader who had a profound influence not only on me, but on thousands of other men and women around the world.

I firmly believe that every organization and every profession needs leaders who inspire others to achieve greatness. There are many such leaders in the internal audit profession, and they are often outstanding internal auditors who inevitably become trusted advisors to management and their boards. So, what are inspirational leaders and what sets them apart from others who serve in leadership roles? Let's face it, there are entire libraries of books, articles, videos, slides, and courses on leadership promising to show you how to become a situational leader, a servant leader, a level-five leader, an authentic leader, or a diamond model leader. It's almost a cliché. Isn't leadership, by any definition, simply leadership?

Trusted advisors certainly are leaders. Their unique positions in their enterprises enable them to connect with management and employees throughout the organization. These leaders seize the opportunities to impart insights and advice in a way that motivates change. But there's another quality that sets these leaders apart: they have the capacity to inspire. They are inspirational change agents!

What differentiates an inspiring leader from one who simply holds a leadership role? I believe that we instinctively recognize when we are being inspired. I certainly recognize when I'm in the presence of an inspirational leader. The leaders I mentioned at the beginning of this chapter had the ability to reach deep inside me and tap into something I didn't know was there. They made me want to grow and achieve far beyond what I thought were my capabilities. It's not that they sat around all day delivering inspiring pep talks. Who has time for that? But just by opening my eyes to opportunities, painting a vision of what the future could be, and conveying their confidence in my abilities, they convinced me that I should take a different path than I might have imagined. Though not each of the inspirational leaders I referenced was an internal auditor, those who were had the same impact in their internal audit capacities.

Inspirational leaders, at least the ones I know, are dripping with charisma—a trait *Psychology Today* defines as the ability to attract, charm, and influence people, often evidenced by confidence, exuberance, optimism, a ready smile, expressive body language, and a friendly, passionate voice.[1] They can rivet you with conversation. They live life in color and they open your eyes to color as well. They are never content to be average or just okay. They strive to be the very best they can be, and they want those around them to be their very best.

Inspirational leaders also are able to articulate a vision and unite people to bring that vision to life. "Inspirational leaders help others rally around a unified and shared vision for what success looks like," says Paul Sobel. "They inspire others to pursue and achieve what they may not have thought possible." These leaders seek to change the trajectory of the business, whereas management may be focused on maintaining the status quo or inclined to embrace modest change. Inspirational leaders are willing to take risks and sacrifice for their vision, inspiring others to join them. No one wants to be left on the side of the tracks when the train is leaving the station.

Aileen Madden sees inspirational internal audit leaders as possessing certain characteristics, such as honesty, transparency, integrity, credibility, and respect. "If you always deal in the truth, act with integrity in all you do, demonstrate your knowledge and expertise without being patronizing or overbearing, and treat people as you expect to be treated, you will show people you can be trusted," Madden says. "You will inspire others by your actions, as well as by your words."

Leaders like this are extraordinary. Maybe I was only lucky enough to encounter two or three of them in my career, but I know this, when I moved on from their service, I was a better internal auditor and a better person than when I started. I can look back as much as 30 years later and admire their style and ability to inspire others.

INSIDE THE MIND OF THE INSPIRATIONAL LEADER

Becoming an inspirational leader starts with a mindset. These leaders think in ways that inspire themselves and enable them to inspire others.

They are fully committed to innovation and they approach situations in a "rethink and reframe" mode. Simply keeping the assembly line moving is no longer success. In today's fast-paced economy, companies rely on leaders who seek innovation in every undertaking, who rethink every problem and opportunity, and who reframe them from a variety of angles. These leaders tend to outmaneuver the competition and ensure that complacency is not part of the corporate culture. They also make business fun again.

This embedded drive to innovate is connected to their intellectual curiosity, an attribute I discussed earlier. Trusted advisors who are intellectually curious demonstrate a commitment to learning, are inquisitive, and continuously seek new ideas and insights. We've heard the stories of Newton's experience with the apple, leading to his theory on gravitation,[2] and Archimedes' famous bath, during which he discovered a way to determine the volume of an object.[3] These stories may have been embellished over time, but they make an important point. Inspirational leaders know that new ideas and new ways of thinking can come from many places, so they remain alert to sources others may overlook.

The inspirational leaders I have known also have a sense of humor. They can see the humor in everyday situations and are willing to set aside business for a moment to enjoy a laugh with colleagues. That doesn't mean they don't take their tasks or others seriously. They know how to balance a light-hearted moment in any given situation.

People want to feel inspired. They want more from their jobs than just a paycheck; they want a purpose. Tracy L. Massey, director of internal audit and chief risk officer for WEA Insurance Corporation, points out, "Employees need to have a desire to do what they are doing and to be where they are in order for them to have open minds, think outside their normal work, and take the initiative to improve. They also want to know that what they do means something to the company." Inspirational leaders recognize that, and they embody and promote the spirit and soul of the enterprise. This is not just a façade. Inspirational leaders are authentic to the core—the computer term WYSIWYG (what you see is what you get) applies perfectly to them. They simply understand that organizations should stand for something other than outputs or profit, and they take it upon themselves to shape and model the values that define that larger purpose.

Respondents to the AEC survey used inspiring words to describe the thought patterns of inspirational internal auditors. They described their "love for and personal/professional satisfaction from audit work, through all the ups and downs." They ascribed to them a passion for the profession and a desire to advocate for it, educating others on its important role. And they mentioned these leaders' commitment to excellence—in the organization, in the internal audit function, and in themselves. As one noted, "I find that auditors who are committed to being the best typically are the best." Those who remember Bill Bishop will recall that he routinely asked audiences to stand up and recite the words "I'm proud to be an internal auditor." In fact, he would even apply a faux IIA tattoo to his forearm that he would reveal to audiences to humorously drive home the point.

CONVERTING THOUGHTS TO ACTIONS

Although the thought patterns of inspirational leaders are important—they are a key element in what causes them to inspire others to greatness—on their own, they are of value only to the thinker. To inspire others, they have to be coupled with productive, purposeful actions.

Through research and experience, I have found a vast array of behaviors exhibited by outstanding internal auditors and other inspirational leaders. I'll focus on the ones I believe to be especially pertinent. Inspirational leaders:

- **Share their experience**. Experience is often hard-won and leaves scars. To save others from going through the same ordeals, inspirational leaders share what they've learned and fill in the context of how they learned it and why it matters. Their listeners may not take their advice, but these leaders are staunch supporters of the wisdom of leading a horse to water, whether or not it drinks.

- **Let others lead**. They do not necessarily take an entirely hands-off approach, but they do create opportunities for others to exercise autonomy. No one is born with full mastery of leadership skills; it takes practice to wield them appropriately. Inspirational leaders not only create opportunities for team members to take charge, they recognize their effective use of leadership acumen. They know that the unique viewpoint that accompanies the leadership role helps these individuals connect their personal goals to business goals.

- **Coach and train their people to greatness**. They are constantly on the hunt for talent; consequently, they have a tendency to find it. Then they evaluate these future leaders' potential, determine their strengths and weaknesses, and guide them in building on the strengths and shoring up the weaker areas. They take great satisfaction in the success of those they have mentored. This eye on the future is critical to the continued relevance of the profession. As Paul Sobel notes, "We are a profession that is only as good as its people. Those who lead must leave a legacy of future leaders. It's not so much about what we accomplish in our jobs today, it's about what those we train and inspire can accomplish in the future."

- **Build teams and promote teamwork.** Inspirational leaders build communities by connecting with others in meaningful and unique ways, whether virtually or in person. But they don't stop at just connecting; they work with others to accomplish goals across geographic and organizational boundaries. Collaboration sometimes runs into roadblocks because conventional reward systems reinforce a "what's in it for me" mindset. Inspirational leaders bypass those roadblocks by modeling collaborative behavior and demonstrating how it can lead to greater, not less, success. I believe strongly that the ability to build and work through successful teams is critical to inspirational leaders, and I am just as convinced of the truth of its corollary: the one characteristic that will ensure you will never be an inspirational leader is ego. If you focus more on yourself than others, you will fall short.

- **Employ purposeful emotion.** Because of the imperative to maintain objectivity and independence, some internal auditors may be perceived as emotionless machines. As we know, that is far from the truth. We are human beings and we experience all the same emotions as anyone. Inspirational leaders also experience emotions, but they contain and control them to a significant degree, knowing that emotion is more impactful when it is rarely seen. But these leaders also know that, while emotion can be expressed at appropriate moments, it achieves its purpose only if it is clearly seen to be sincere, honest, and uncalculated. General Colin Powell articulated 13 rules for leadership, one of which is: "Get mad, then get over it."[4]

- **Lead through culture**. Culture is an organization's enduring asset, significant beyond a single leader's impact. I often embrace the definition that culture is "how we do things around here." Inspirational leaders seek to build a culture that is based on values, is energetic, embraces transparency, and recognizes accomplishments. They strive to ensure that "things are done around here the right way." One of our survey respondents recognized the role inspirational leaders play when she pointed out that they foster a culture of continuous improvement.

- **Face challenges**. Inspirational leaders deal honestly with challenges, keeping employees informed of both good news and bad. They focus on what can be done and develop a plan. One of the AEC survey respondents noted the need for courage in dealing with work challenges: "To be effective, you need to set aside the hierarchy of who you are speaking to. You have to be confident enough to 'speak truth to power' without fear." She went on to say that, once internal auditors land in the CAE role, they must have the courage of their convictions and "be willing to walk if the situation requires." People reveal much more about themselves in the way they handle adversity than success.

- **Earn and extend trust**. It's no surprise this one would end up on my list. Trusted advisors, by their very identity, earn trust, but they also trust others. They understand that when employees feel empowered to do their best work, it inspires them to excel at reaching their goals. Ultimately, the workplace becomes permeated with trust, led by someone who has their best interests at heart.

GETTING STARTED

I mentioned earlier that no one is born a leader. I do believe, though, that some people have a genetic predisposition to use their innate talents to lead. To have impact, these natural leaders must recognize their talent and be willing to leverage it. I also fervently believe that even those not genetically predisposed to lead can become inspirational leaders. It may take a bit more effort and perseverance, but the journey and the destination can be richly rewarding both for the leader and those being led.

If you have what it takes to be an inspirational leader, you have a gift—and a responsibility. If you don't share your abilities, you've wasted an opportunity. You must use them in the best, most productive way you can and recognize that the things you say and do (or don't say and do) will have greater impact than the statements and actions of others. In fact, they will ultimately define your success and your legacy: with ability comes responsibility.

I also mentioned at the start of this chapter that there are endless bookshelves filled with content on how to become a better leader. Many of those volumes are quite insightful and helpful. But with leadership, sometimes just reading about it is not enough. It is often more powerful to study the behaviors of individuals you believe to be good leaders. History is full of them. Martin Luther King Jr., Gandhi, Teddy Roosevelt, and Winston Churchill are some of my own personal heroes. Consider how these people are perceived decades after their death. They are still admired as strong, charismatic, and effective leaders who changed history and inspired hundreds of thousands of followers.

But maybe you would feel more in tune with leaders who are a bit more approachable. Anyone who knows me knows I am a huge fan of the University of Alabama football program, the Crimson Tide. That program has experienced a long and consistent history of success, attributable in large part to its good fortune in having two of college football's most inspiring and accomplished head coaches: the late Paul "Bear" Bryant and, more recently, Nick Saban.

Bear Bryant believed in accepting responsibility for errors and delegating credit for successes. He recognized talent and valued character, and he knew that motivating his players called for him to know what made each one of them tick. Bryant refused to surround himself with "yes men." In fact, he was so invested in getting the straight story about his coaching that he would ask friends to "scout" him—observe and report to him on his performance. And, most importantly, he emphasized playing as a team, not as a group of talented individuals. He explained, "People who are in it for their own good are individualists. They don't share the same heartbeat that makes a team so great. A great unit, whether it be football or any organization, shares the same heartbeat."[5]

Nick Saban was selected by *Fortune* magazine as one of its 2016 World's Greatest Leaders.[6] He inspires his team to "do their job," focusing on one play at a time, as the most important area of focus at that moment—not becoming distracted by the score, or what victory will feel like, or what statistics they are racking up. He encourages them to focus only on what they have to do in that play.[7] This echoes the approach of many inspirational leaders. A constant focus on the big picture and the future may make people feel hopeful and engaged, but it's equally important to achieve excellence in the short term.

I would argue that the inspirational leadership lessons from these two football coaches certainly equal, and probably surpass, much of the leadership advice handed out by business pundits. Perhaps sports analogies don't work for you. That's fine. It doesn't matter which leaders inspire and motivate you, the point is to find those people and study their words and actions. Research their mistakes as well; you can learn a lot by examining errors in judgment of leaders.

Why should you make such an effort to learn and adopt inspirational leadership characteristics? One very practical answer for internal auditors, as noted by Aileen Madden, is that it will help you get desired results. "You need to be able to inspire your client to improve the areas of weakness you've identified," she said.

Karen Begelfer also recognizes the power of inspiration in getting things done. She said, "An auditor's job is to advocate for what is right, even when it might be unpopular or difficult to achieve. Auditors who demonstrate inspirational leadership can quickly get others on board and working together to improve, which leads to faster and superior value delivery." Outstanding internal auditors don't consider their work done when they present the final report; they are satisfied only when the results outlined in the report are achieved. Sometimes it takes a bit of inspiration to make that happen. In another of his 13 Rules, General Powell observes, "A dream doesn't become a reality through magic; it takes sweat, determination and hard work."[8]

IBM recently asked 1,700 CEOs in 64 countries what they want from their leadership ranks. The top three traits are: an intense focus on customer needs, collaboration with colleagues, and being able to inspire.[9] *Harvard Business Review* studied leadership competencies by gathering 360-degree feedback data from nearly 50,000 leaders assessed by a half-million colleagues. The data indicate that an ability to inspire creates the highest levels of employee engagement and commitment; it is the factor most subordinates identify when asked what they would most like to have in their leader.[10]

But if data seem too clinical and analytical to think about something as emotive as inspiration, consider this anecdotal story in which Tracy Massey describes a moment in her own organization when an inspirational leader made a huge difference in employee motivation. At the time of this event, the company had been struggling to rebound from a long period marked by failure to innovate, lackluster leadership, loss of customers, and financial downturn. A staff meeting was called where the organization's leaders shared the declining first-quarter financial results and discussed the need to turn the trend around. The last executive to speak was the CFO, who had already been identified as the next CEO.

> "He emphasized that every single one of us has an obligation to make needed changes," Massey recalls. "He expressed his belief in us and our ability to make it happen." He then referenced a football play—the sweep—that the Green Bay Packers were known for. He explained the steps of the play, the positions of the players involved in the play, and statistics on how successful that play was for the team. He referenced one particular position, the fullback, who was responsible for the key block in the play. If that player didn't do his job, the sweep wouldn't be successful. In the early 1960s, when the Packers dominated football and the sweep became the team's signature play, the fullback position was filled, brilliantly, by Hall of Famer Paul Hornung.
>
> The CFO then shared the perspective of Packers coach, the late Vince Lombardi, on the play: Lombardi always

held that the sweep was just a play, nothing magical to it. However, he also believed that, with attitude and execution, the right play can come to personify the heart and soul of an entire team and make the whole enterprise excel. "As the CFO told this story, his excitement and passion about the play and his respect for Coach Lombardi were transferred to the staff," Massey describes. "We were right there with him. The room was quiet as he concluded with, 'Who here wants to be our Hornung?'"

"In one simple moment," Massey adds, "he turned a roomful of individual employees into a team."

Inspirational leaders tend to motivate a drive to action and results. The best results are not those arrived at haphazardly, nor are they based on sparse information or shallow evaluation. Effective results rely on the ability to think critically about the situation and data before us, an attribute that we'll explore in the next chapter.

PROFESSIONAL ATTRIBUTES

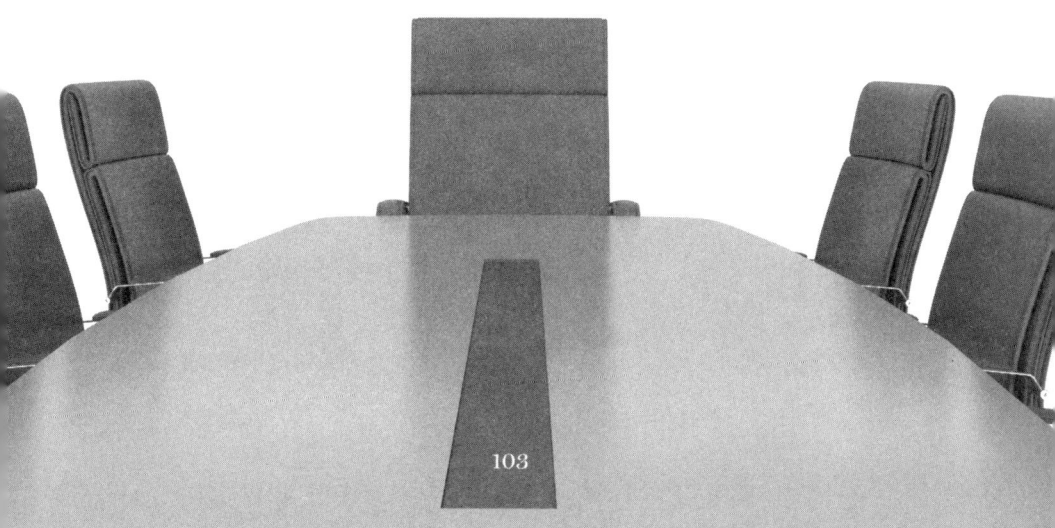

CRITICAL THINKERS

ONE OF MY most frustrating experiences as an audit supervisor and, eventually, as an audit executive was to sit down with internal auditors or audit teams who had generated vast amounts of data and audit evidence, but were lost when it came time to make sense out of it. While my frustration materialized at the end of the process, the internal auditors' frustration had been building for weeks or even months. They often crafted outstanding risk-based audit plans that served as the basis for their engagement, and often leveraged intellectual curiosity in gathering the information in their workpapers. However, they were frequently stumped when it came to identifying and connecting the critical dots. They had not developed, or were not leveraging, critical thinking skills.

Critical thinking is taking often vast amounts of information gathered through intellectual curiosity and creating a well-reasoned, thorough, and nuanced understanding of the situation and appropriate recommendations.

Intellectual curiosity and critical thinking are connected, no doubt about it. It is unlikely for someone to have one trait without the other. For example, what sort of chef would gather the ingredients for a gourmet meal and then do nothing with them? And the chef who tries to create an impressive dish out of few, no, or substandard ingredients is unlikely to produce anything memorable (or even edible). The two traits go together—to continue our culinary metaphor and to quote the inimitable Forrest Gump—like peas and carrots.

The AEC survey respondents recognized the distinction between the two and placed more emphasis on the importance of critical thinking in the practice of internal audit than intellectual curiosity. Only 19 percent chose intellectual curiosity among their top three attributes of outstanding internal auditors, while a hefty 49 percent selected critical thinking. Clearly they are both important. But it's equally clear we would be well advised to build on the base of intellectual curiosity we discussed earlier to expand our skills into critical thinking.

DEFINING THE TERM

Critical thinking is not an easily captured concept, as becomes evident once you begin trying to pin down a definition. Being a person who always believes in going to the experts when I have a question, I immediately consulted the National Council for Excellence in Critical Thinking (NCECT). In summary, the NCECT defines critical thinking as the "intellectually disciplined process of actively and skillfully conceptualizing, applying, analyzing, synthesizing, and/or evaluating information gathered from, or generated by, observation, experience, reflection, reasoning, or communication, as a guide to belief and action."[1] It refers to the intellectual values on which it is based—among them, clarity, accuracy, precision, consistency, relevance, and sound evidence—and notes that these transcend subject matter areas.

The NCECT's authors further describe critical thinking as consisting of two components: skills in generating and processing information and belief, and the habit of using those skills to guide behavior. They also reinforce the distinction between critical thinking and intellectual curiosity by pointing out that critical thinking is not solely an exercise in acquiring and retaining information; it requires the information to be treated a certain way, the skills to be used continually, and the results to be accepted.

Patty Miller, retired partner at Deloitte & Touche LLP and now owner of PKMiller Risk Consulting, LLC, contributed to the development of the joint Deloitte-IIA course on critical thinking for internal auditors. She refers to critical thinking as "using reasoning and logic, not emotion, to evaluate information and consider alternatives." But, she adds, "You must do all that objectively and with an open mind so you come to a reasonable conclusion."

In the context of internal auditing, I believe critical thinking is the ability to take information or a set of circumstances, consider the inherent challenges or weaknesses, identify deviation from acceptable criteria, and then do a root cause analysis to fully understand why something did or didn't happen.

Regardless of the exact definition or professional context, having a solid understanding of critical thinking and putting it into practice are increasingly important in career advancement, with the mere mention of critical thinking in job postings doubling between 2009 and 2014, according to Indeed.com.[2] But just because bosses are asking for critical thinkers doesn't mean they are clear on what they actually want. Some employers complain that new graduates cannot solve problems or draw inferences on complex issues. However, those same employers are unable to define exactly what skills they consider "musts" for critical thinking.[3] Perhaps they don't truly want critical thinkers at all. Linda Elder, educational psychologist and prominent authority on critical thinking, suggests that they may really want well-trained problem solvers, not critical thinkers, especially in the lower ranks. Why? Because critical thinkers tend to challenge the status quo—not always a trait at the top of bosses' must-have lists.

Not all employers are so reluctant to take on challenges, though. There is certainly enough evidence to suggest that mastery of self-directed, self-disciplined, self-monitored, and self-corrective thinking will always be welcome in most workplaces. For successful internal audit departments, and those internal auditors who seek to be trusted advisors, it is imperative.

CRITICAL THINKING AND INTERNAL AUDIT

But don't take it just from me. The AEC survey respondents said they see elements of critical thinking as primary attributes of outstanding internal auditors:

- "Audit results and assessments are no longer pass/fail. Judgment is needed to understand criticality and the potential impacts of issues, along with the impact of risk tolerances and/or mitigating controls."

- "Creative problem solving—the application of best practices from diverse sources to create fresh solutions—is a must."

- "Critical thinking is important because it is systematic and disciplined, two traits that are at the heart of the definition of internal auditing. Many auditors succeed or fail on their ability (or inability) to be systematic and disciplined."

I think they nailed it. If we wish to be trusted advisors, we have to live up to the expectation that we can evaluate issues and fully understand why something has happened. It's a prerequisite to correcting the problem and ensuring it doesn't happen again. We must not only diagnose what happened but also interpret the information (some we may only intuit) and offer a prognosis on what *could* happen. As internal audits become more complex and we are asked to assess functions that are not traditional areas of focus for our profession, such as organizational culture, critical thinking will become an absolutely vital skill for those seeking to become trusted advisors.

Patty Miller captures succinctly why critical thinking is so important for internal auditors. "People rely on our work and our conclusions. The board, the audit committee, executive management, and sometimes even regulators and outside parties are relying on us to be thorough and objective in coming to a conclusion." If we are unable to "cut to the chase" and succinctly articulate the crux of complex issues, they won't have time for us.

The fact that people rely on internal audit's assessments speaks directly to the value equation—what internal audit contributes to company success. "Critical thinking dramatically increases the value internal audit provides to its stakeholders," says Shawn Tebben, vice president of internal audit at Vail Resorts. "Auditors skilled in critical thinking don't get stuck in blindly following an audit program or checklist. They are agile in how they approach a project and are confident in adjusting as new information is learned or analyzed. The end result is that they get to the root of issues and work with management to solve for those issues rather than just treating the symptoms."

As an example, Tebben cites an internal audit project involving inventory. "Financial reporting-related controls were tested as part of Sarbanes-Oxley and management was skeptical that internal audit could bring any real value to them," she says. "Although management's net variances were well below industry averages, the audit team analyzed data and uncovered some large absolute variances that got management's attention. By using the business's own data, the team was able to gain buy-in that the project could help them better manage inventory. In the end, a number of operational improvements were implemented by management, along with ongoing monitoring using the same analysis the audit team used."

Critical thinking has been called a domain-general thinking skill[4]— perfect for internal auditors who engage with varied disciplines and become familiar enough with them to provide an informed assessment. It has been classified as very important in the current knowledge economy,[5] because it enables dealing quickly and effectively with change and supports the integration of diverse sources of knowledge, brings clarity to complex issues, and promotes creativity.

BEING A SKEPTIC

Somewhere along the way, skepticism was imbued with negative connotations. It's not uncommon to hear people say, somewhat dismissively, "Don't be such a skeptic," in response to expressions of rational doubt. But it is yet another irony in that skepticism is an innately beneficial human characteristic and often a matter of self-preservation. We in internal audit need to reclaim the trait of skepticism and polish its reputation. After all, my own organization's research paper on behaviors of internal auditors states quite clearly, "Professional skepticism is an essential element of the internal auditor's package of skills and an ingredient that must be continually developed and 'listened to.'"[6]

If you are an internal auditor, even with only a few years of experience, I would bet that somewhere along the way you've heard a response like this: "Trust me, this is what happened. Why do you keep asking me the same questions when I've already given you the answers?" But we know it's not simply a matter of trust—it's about verification, so that trust can be properly placed.

This process of verification is so important to John J. Lind, director of risk management for the Brookshire Grocery Company, that it influenced his AEC survey selection of critical thinking as the most important attribute of outstanding internal auditors. He explains, "Critical thinking was at the top of my list for one large reason: the concept of professional skepticism. A primary setback I have seen and continue to see throughout my career arises when people settle for the first feasible answer as opposed to looking for the most correct or fully correct answer. They're lacking a certain ability and discipline to critically think through the information." He relates a time when he was managing an audit of on-time shipping performance in the manufacturing division of a company.

> "One of the risks we were assessing was the accuracy of performance metrics; specifically, how often the right product was shipped to the right customer at the right time. The fact that a financial bonus was paid to manufacturing leaders when the on-time shipping performance was above 95 percent augmented the risk. The shipping performance was historically in the 60 percent to 80 percent range, until a new VP came on board and, within months, it rose to be consistently above 95 percent. The staff auditor interviewed manufacturing leaders and personnel, looked at supporting sales and shipping records, recalculated the on-time shipping percentage, and concluded that the increase in the on-time shipping performance was accurate. The incentive was appropriately paid.
>
> I reviewed his work and, during our conversations, it became apparent that the auditor did not adequately question or analyze the information. My team discovered that the manufacturing leaders had made a change in the way they calculated on-time shipping performance when the new VP had come on board. They switched

from calculating on a product SKU basis to a product category basis. The new measure allowed the manufacturing group to claim 100 percent performance when the appropriate number of products was shipped, even if the products weren't what the customer ordered. When we recalculated the percentage by the original SKU method, performance fell back down to the original 60 percent to 80 percent range. This was deemed a more significant measure because it reflected the customer's desire to get not just the right number of products, but the right products themselves. The lesson for the auditor was that he was too quick to accept the manufacturing group's perspective without more critical thought and professional skepticism."

I talked about skepticism earlier in the book, noting that it is often modified with the adjectives *healthy* or *credible* to highlight a key distinction: appropriate use of questioning to see beyond the superficial versus an automatic and cynical predisposition to distrust. One of the AEC survey respondents applied this characterization by defining skepticism as "a healthy dose of doubt, coupled with curiosity, which could lead to uncovering areas of risk exposure or fraud." It would be arrogant to think that internal auditors are not susceptible to being misled by information that is sensational, popular, or entertaining. But I would argue that outstanding internal auditors are also more likely to delve deeper to get to the truth of the matter.

Patty Miller recalls a situation from many years ago that nicely illustrates the value of professional skepticism and the damage that may occur when it is not applied rigorously. An audit was being conducted at an organization that had a policy of requiring approval signatures on purchases based on the amount of the purchase. One element of the audit was to test whether those signatures were being gathered correctly and consistently. The internal auditor spoke to the purchasing clerk, who explained that, because the organization was small and "everybody knew everybody," they didn't deal in formality. The purchasing clerk said he saw everything before it went into the system and that he was very familiar with who was authorized to buy what. So based on this statement, without talking to his audit manager or anyone else, the auditor completed the test without exception, although many purchases were not approved per policy. He didn't exercise any skepticism whatsoever, much less enough to ask himself, "Is this enough information to know the current practice is okay? Should I talk to someone else before closing it out?" Fortunately, when the testing failure was found and the purchases were retested, no fraud was identified, just a control failure that, at least in this case, didn't lead to unauthorized purchases. But it could have. A healthy dose of skepticism would have been well in order.

Effective professional skepticism requires a combination of interpersonal and technical skills. Interpersonal skills support the ability to read and communicate effectively with others, and to ask probing questions that will uncover pertinent facts. Technical skills involve audit-specific expertise, industry knowledge, objectivity, and reasoning that enable analysis of those facts. I wrote about these two skillsets in *Lessons Learned on the Audit Trail* as being necessary to earning trusted advisor status. There is a certain irony that those who exercise skepticism rather than blind trust are often the ones who truly become trusted advisors.

OBSTACLES TO THINKING CRITICALLY

In any profession, thinking critically requires conscious thought and discipline. For most of us, it does not come easily or without practice, nor without the need to surmount obstacles.

Perhaps the most challenging obstacle for internal auditors is dealing with bias. One of our AEC survey respondents called out that challenge specifically: "A fatal flaw I see in some auditors is the inability to understand that their personal opinion doesn't matter. Having an actual objective mindset is crucial. And difficult to teach."

Patty Miller also notes the importance of avoiding bias: "You must go into an audit with an open mind, not drawing immediate conclusions based on your prior experience. If you've audited an area several times and it always had strong controls, and if you assume that means that every time it is audited it will have those strong controls, you have blinders on. Good internal auditors always realize there could be an issue, there could be a problem. We can't afford to rely solely on prior experience and disregard or dismiss signs and symptoms of a problem."

Her comments touch on another obstacle to critical thinking: familiarity—when an internal auditor expects something to be a certain way because it has always been that way. Familiarity with a client can result in a preconceived notion about an upcoming audit's outcome. It can make internal auditors less willing to find or acknowledge discrediting information about an organization, department, or individual. It blocks the ability to think critically about what's actually before us.

Discounting is the phenomenon in which immediate consequences are given greater emphasis than delayed outcomes, especially when those delayed outcomes are uncertain. It is easy to see how this might be reflected in an audit context. Internal auditors may develop recommendations that fail to give full consideration to later possibilities in their desire to address current consequences. Finding a balance between the here and now and future risks is possible only through thinking critically and dispassionately.

Critical thinking is dependent on having complete information. I noted earlier the connection between critical thinking and intellectual curiosity. If there is a failure in the internal auditor's intellectual curiosity—if we neglect to ask why as many times as it takes to get to the root cause—or there's a deficiency in skills or expertise in a certain area, a key risk may be missed or ignored. In my own experience, and from talking to an array of CAEs, the most common areas that fail to make the risk assessment because of internal audit's lack of skills are those related to technology and to business/strategic risks. But there really is no excuse for walking away from these and other critical topics. Where there is a skills gap, the CAE can fill it by hiring the needed talent, co-sourcing, or leveraging expertise from elsewhere in the organization—anything to ensure that the proper degree of thought and scrutiny is applied to business-critical issues.

Failure to follow through is another stumbling block within the exercise of critical thinking. I believe that crafting the recommendations in an audit report is one of the more challenging aspects of the job. It is sometimes more exhilarating to identify a failure or problem than to figure out how to keep it from happening again. The frustrated internal auditors I spoke about at the beginning of this chapter started out thoroughly enjoying the challenge of identifying and documenting problems. However, they were ultimately faced with a mountain of puzzle pieces, and they couldn't figure out how all the pieces fit together—or what the resulting picture portrayed.

To be trusted advisors, we must be riveted on identifying the best solutions, not just the problems. That's where the real value of internal audit comes in. Our clients usually know when they have problems. What they need is to fully understand the causes and be afforded recommendations and insights that yield the best solutions. And the best solutions result from critical thinking.

Sometimes the most stubborn of challenges to critical thinking are within us—our own perceptions, shortcomings, and beliefs. Anyone who has an inherent lack of respect for reasoning or evidence, or is unwilling to listen to others, is unlikely to be able to think critically. Intellectual arrogance ("I already know the answer") and intellectual laziness ("Good enough is good enough") will also undermine attempts to think in a disciplined manner.

And in some cases, critical thinking is stymied simply because people don't know what it is or whether it is part of their responsibilities. "You have to make sure people understand the concept of critical thinking and what the related expectations are for them," Patty Miller advises. "They need to understand that taking an 'I'm sure it will be okay' attitude will most likely mean you will not identify an issue, delaying any solution."

Critical thinking is, well, critical to success in internal auditing. But it does not exist in a vacuum. We can't just sit around and think critically; we must be thinking *about* something, using information and experience to shape ideas and conclusions. Our thinking must be supported by extensive and profound technical skills in business, industry, and technology.

TECHNICAL EXPERTISE

THE EXTRAORDINARY OPPORTUNITY I had at the U.S. Postal Service—helping to build the audit arm of the Office of Inspector General—was a chance to recruit the best professionals with technical expertise to take on our new mission. We recruited hundreds of auditors from across government and the corporate sector to constitute what amounted to a newly formed internal audit function of one of the largest and most complex business enterprises in the world. Looking back, it was enlightening to observe the skills and characteristics that quickly set the most successful of our new recruits apart. It wasn't audit skills or writing skills, as one might expect. Those who quickly distinguished themselves in the eyes of those we audited were the men and women who either possessed or quickly cultivated knowledge of the business, industry expertise, and technology skills. They emerged the fastest as the most trusted advisors from among their peers.

The value of technical skills or acumen has been recognized for centuries. As far back as the mid-1400s, men began to consciously aspire to and work toward becoming polymaths, or masters of many trades. They accumulated a broad base of knowledge, acquired skills in multiple fields, became fluent in several languages, amassed a profound understanding of philosophy and the scientific teachings of the day, appreciated and even created literature and art, and developed their athletic prowess. Leonardo da Vinci is considered the quintessential representative of the type. So significantly did these men represent the spirit of the age that, over time, they were assigned the name of the historical period itself. They were Renaissance men.

In limiting the term to men only, I am not exhibiting a personal bias. The sad fact is that women of the period generally did not have the opportunity to acquire and demonstrate the required knowledge and skills. There were Renaissance women, but they were certainly less noted by historians.

So, you might ask, where am I going with this? In this chapter, I discuss the body of knowledge (business acumen, industry expertise, and technology insight) that internal auditors must master if they are to become trusted advisors—our profession's Renaissance people. Like those from the Renaissance era, expertise must be broad. An internal auditor with business acumen may navigate organizational politics well, but without industry knowledge, risks specific to a company's core business may not be recognized. An internal auditor who knows technology backward and forward, but who does not know how to progress a proposal for a new audit management system through the corporate approval process, is likely to watch a great idea wither on the vine. To be a da Vinci, we need proficiency in all three disciplines.

I must confess that this is a conviction I have not always held. When I sought out a survey as part of my research for this book, I considered business acumen, industry expertise, and technology insight as three distinct, if not sometimes overlapping, skillsets. However, it quickly became evident through the survey responses that there are critical interdependencies among what ranks as the top three traits of outstanding internal auditors.

KNOWING THE BUSINESS

Business acumen has a varied definition covering different areas of knowledge and expertise. In my view, business acumen means understanding the common threads in any business: objectives, business plans, general processes, organizational structure and culture, and strategies related to products and services. Although it can be perceived as a fairly generic and high-level knowledge area, it lays the groundwork for a much shorter learning curve in understanding the core processes of a particular industry and company.

Generally speaking, individuals who possess business acumen are perceived to consistently exercise sound judgment and make decisions that result in favorable outcomes. They can assimilate information from an array of sources and use that new knowledge to propose sound strategic alternatives to address issues and problems. They also are always looking ahead trying to foresee opportunities and threats, the better to develop strategies to remain one step ahead of the competition. Possibly most important, they have the ability to see across the many areas of expertise within a company, such as finance, research and development, marketing, and IT; understand how decisions affect each of these areas; and work toward coordinating efforts to ensure shared success. This trait is called "breadth of understanding,"[1] and it was called out specifically in the AEC survey responses as a skill that can be achieved only by conscious effort and one that must be "continuously worked on."

Not only does business acumen encompass understanding differing functional areas, it also means being able to speak to these areas in their own language. Obviously, it doesn't require those in one functional area—say, internal auditors—to be deep technical experts in all the other functional areas within the organization. No one has time for that. But business acumen does require a basic understanding of all areas and each one's unique mission and vocabulary. Of course, understanding the mission and speaking the vocabulary don't necessarily guarantee harmony.

In recent years, an increasing number of companies have designated the CAE position as a rotational assignment. Seasoned executives from within the company are often asked by the CEO or audit committee to assume the role for what is often a three- to five-year assignment. The CAE role is often seen as one that prepares executives to assume positions of greater responsibility within the company in the future. However, the candidates who are asked to take on the CAE role are often tapped based on their business acumen. They assume their new role with years or even decades of experience in the company or industry. In that regard, they are seen by other executives in the company as being prewired as, or to become, trusted advisors.

Organizational politics. Organizational politics are a fact of life in every company—in fact, in every group of human beings, whether it's a social club, a religious institution, a professional association, a school, or a neighborhood. Anywhere humans may pursue their own agendas and self-interests is fertile soil for organizational politics. Navigating these choppy, often dangerous, waters is a specific facet of business acumen and one that is well worth mastering, especially for internal auditors, who must work with a wide range of individuals in the organization while asserting and protecting their objectivity and independence.

Dealing with organizational politics requires an understanding of the formal and informal hierarchies within an organization, the rules, and the players. Armed with this understanding, trusted advisors often apply some of the following basic tactics for navigating organizational politics:

- Rely on facts (data) and always tell the truth.
- Build alliances; help others.
- Admit when you have made a mistake, but also stand up for yourself when you are right.
- Understand the question behind the question; don't immediately accept things as they may appear.
- Find common ground. When possible, be the peacemaker.
- Use good judgment. As one AEC survey respondent pointed out, "There is a bit of art as well as science to being a good auditor. Judgment is on the artistic side."
- Remain vigilant and be prepared to adjust your approach when circumstances change.

Opportunities and challenges. Given the need for internal auditors to work well enterprisewide, understand the concerns and issues of all areas, maintain objectivity, and have a firm grasp on existing and potential risks, it is easy to see why business acumen is crucial. In *Lessons Learned on the Audit Trail*, I identified professional expertise in internal audit areas of concern—governance, risk, and control—as one of the two components of being a trusted advisor. Complementing that with the breadth of understanding inherent in business acumen makes the internal auditor an even more valuable resource, and one whose stature will rise above the rest.

Business acumen will open your eyes to the challenges faced by management and the risks they must navigate. However, here's a word of caution: you will probably develop a good deal more empathy with their situation than you may possess at the moment. There is nothing wrong with that. I've talked many times in this book about putting ourselves in another person's shoes, but there is a risk in too much familiarity, in identifying so closely with others that you may begin to overlook their missteps or make excuses for them. At that point, you have lost objectivity, one of the most fundamental tenets of internal auditing. Don't let yourself get that comfortable.

I believe that trusted advisors are empathetic—not sympathetic. Being too sympathetic with management is a challenge that rotational CAEs frequently have to overcome. The transition from peer to CAE often creates a strain on relationships that were previously untested by scrutiny. The credibility of CAEs who are too close to management based on their prior (and potentially future) relationships as peers will ultimately impair the long-term sustainment of trusted advisor status.

THE INDUSTRY PERSPECTIVE

The definition of industry expertise is fairly obvious. It is more specific than general business acumen and refers to understanding the industry in which your company works, whether it is in manufacturing, marketing, retail, finance, government, education, hospitality, or another. Each industry has its own challenges, regulations, language, and processes. This is particularly pertinent to internal auditors, according to Charles Windeknecht, vice president, internal audit department, Atlas Air Worldwide. "I believe if you understand the concepts of risk and control, you can probably audit anywhere. But there is no question it is helpful in certain industries to have an additional layer of specific understanding. I came to Atlas from another industry sector and learning about our industry has made me a better auditor."

An audit executive for a health-care insurance provider agrees: "As we continue to perform more audits that align with our strategic initiatives, it is becoming more critical that our auditors have more knowledge/expertise of the industry. Having industry expertise allows the auditors to identify and focus on the key risks, so that we continue to meet the needs of management and the audit committee. Being in the health care payer space, there continues to be a great deal of change both within the organization and the regulatory environment, and we need to be able to keep up."

As the Committee of Sponsoring Organizations of the Treadway Commission (COSO) observed, every industry exists to achieve certain objectives, and for those objectives, whatever they may be, there are risks that may hinder their achievement. Industry expertise will help in understanding the objectives, the risks, and the mitigation options.

So will an ability to be flexible, which is especially critical in today's turbulent environment in which risks can materialize without warning. In 1990, when Iraq invaded Kuwait, I was CAE for a large military organization. Suddenly, my carefully crafted audit plans were null and void. Internal auditors who work solely from risk-based annual plans in a volatile environment may be auditing challenges that are no longer pressing. A continuous approach to risk assessment, supporting a continually evolving audit plan and coverage, allows identification of and adaptation to emerging risks. Internal auditors with industry expertise are apt to have a better feel for the sorts of events that could suddenly and irrevocably alter the risk landscape of the company.

Often industry experience may be more important than audit experience. The insurance audit executive indicated that her company often has trouble finding internal auditors with industry experience. To address the gap, the company took another tack. "We hired an associate who did not have audit experience but had worked in our organization in operations for a number of years. This auditor has solid working relationships with operations and continues to work closely with the rest of the audit team to help them understand the business processes and industry jargon. The auditor's in-depth knowledge of the operational process has facilitated effective audits with quality results."

Learning the industry. As I did, many internal auditors will work for several organizations and in different industries over the course of a career. To be successful in a new environment, we must have an appetite for learning. Internal auditors cannot be of value if they don't understand what the business is and how it operates. It is imperative to identify and tap sources of information—formal and informal—to become more knowledgeable. Charles Windeknecht found his: "One of my best tools is to be an observer at the daily operations meeting, during which Ops goes over all the flights and other operational issues for the previous 12 hours. Listening to the discussion helped me learn the terminology and the day-to-day situations our industry faces. This is important because it enables me to recognize which occurrences are anomalies as opposed to business as usual, so I can focus on the facts—what happened, what caused it, and what we did about it—instead of overreacting."

I have run across several instances in my career when I realized I needed to ramp up my industry expertise. During those years when we were building a new audit function at the U.S. Postal Service, I developed a good understanding of its core processes: accepting, processing, and delivering mail. Then I went to the Tennessee Valley Authority, a large, complex utility organization—about as far removed from mail processing as it is possible to go. Suddenly I needed to learn about generating and distributing electric power. I immediately signed up for appropriate classes and hit the books. Years later, when I came to The IIA, I knew a great deal about internal auditing and serving the profession, but I was new to association management. I needed to learn how professional not-for-profit associations operate and the leading practices in the field. I joined the American Society of Association Executives and started going to events and reading extensively. Internal auditors are not alone in needing to gain a profound understanding of their industry; anyone who wishes to excel must apply themselves to learning until they have an almost innate feel for the core business, opportunities, and risks of their industry.

Those who fail to acquire deep knowledge will face a fallout in respect, credibility, and, ultimately, trust. As I mentioned at the beginning of this chapter, when I was at the Postal Service, we assembled a staff of almost 700 people in just five years, the majority of whom had little or no background in postal operations or even a field marginally similar. Consequently, many faced a steep learning curve and a number of hurdles. We were in the position of having to send into a processing/

distribution center people who were entirely unfamiliar with the complexities or pressures involved in moving almost 40 percent of the world's mail. We simply didn't have expertise in the core processes and, because of that, we lacked the knowledge to apply critical thinking to industry-specific issues. Until we could establish expertise, we weren't able to add value.

Calling in reinforcements. As a team, we ultimately did learn the industry and became increasingly effective in successfully under-taking most audit engagements. But even with our expanded range of knowledge, we knew we needed help when dealing with very sensitive or technical areas. For example, the Postal Service used some fairly complex economic models to set rates—so complex, in fact, that the service had its own staff of economists to build those models. I knew that when my team of auditors was brought in to audit that area of the organization, we were going to be well out of our comfort zone. How could we assess those models when we didn't have that expertise? We brought in our own experts. We contracted with two economists who joined me in select meetings. One would sit on my right side, the other on my left. Almost literally and figuratively they were my right and left arms. Their presence gave us immense confidence and credibility.

The lesson is: when expertise is lacking, whether in an industry overall or in a specific process, secure it by any and all other means. Bringing in help will not harm your reputation as a trusted advisor. On the contrary, it will elevate it. It will show others you are aware of your limitations, honest enough to admit them to others, and smart enough to figure out how to get the job done anyway. Even trusted advisors need trusted advisors.

CAPITALIZING ON TECHNOLOGY

At the risk of dating myself, I confess that when I became an internal auditor, my colleagues and I were taught to audit "around the computer." Yes, there was a time when not all information assets were digitized, analyzed, stored, and manipulated in a computer, so it was possible to conduct in-depth audits without having to delve into IT. Clearly, that day has passed. In fact, there's been a 180-degree shift, and it is difficult to imagine an audit without significant interaction with IT.

Tim Kenny, general auditor for Freddie Mac, sees the dominance of technology as very clear: "While credit risk is our largest risk, our company, and I would imagine many others, spend big dollars on IT strategy and initiatives to enable key business strategies. IT costs and initiative spend are significant components of our administrative expense budget annually. It follows that certain IT risks—disaster recovery and business continuity; information security, privacy, and cyberthreats; technology change management; and identity and access management—are among the highest inherent risks to our company."

The pervasiveness of technology and data is of critical importance to Martin Silverman, director of internal audit at the New York Independent System Operator (NYISO), which operates wholesale markets to manage the flow of electricity across New York: "Markets and the energy grid—especially important to my company—are run on technology. Having complete and accurate data is a huge factor in terms of internal audit being effective and knowing whether controls are operating effectively. We can talk to people and that's useful, but data is the acid test. It can confirm or refute what people say."

Internal audit and technology. Occasionally, I will hear someone say that internal auditors tend to fall behind other professionals in the area of innovation. Certainly, scientists, engineers, and computer programmers may aggressively accept and take advantage of IT. But over the past two decades, internal audit has adopted and made excellent use of new technology, such as audit management systems and data mining and analysis. Hoss Behzadi, director of audit and evaluation for the Canadian Dairy Commission, tells how his team's knowledge of plant technology and best practices enabled it to recommend testing and weighing equipment that helped the plant staff identify the area of certain losses. That, in turn, helped to eliminate 6 percent of lost raw material. Such a quantifiable contribution cannot be overstated in proving internal audit's value.

We must continue down the technology path and, in fact, pick up the pace. Martin Silverman points to the huge amounts of data analyzed via continuous auditing and the advantages of letting the computer sift through it quickly. "It gives us an opportunity we never had before," he said. "Otherwise, it's needles in haystacks."

Certainly, respondents to the AEC survey respect the advantages of technology and see it as a key attribute of outstanding internal auditors, ranging from the fairly specific recommendation of proficiency in "audit analytical tools with some programming knowledge for script development" to the more general and often repeated call for enhanced knowledge and use of data analytics.

Technology benefits. It's hard to argue with this. And, really, why would we? Why wouldn't we want to explore and leverage these and other new technologies? Technology clearly brings significant benefits to the workplace, and also some emerging risks. Automation can enhance productivity, enable people to do things more efficiently, and result in more accurate outcomes. Increased efficiency equates to cost savings, as it supports getting things done faster and with fewer resources. The ability to store massive amounts of data in easily searchable formats, further enhanced by cloud computing, saves time and space and spares the environment.

Technology allows employees to collaborate in real time across great distances, and mobile devices make it possible for people to work anytime and almost anywhere—expanding their productivity and providing them a degree of flexibility that makes them more satisfied with their jobs. Enterprises with leading-edge systems and a reputation for innovation tend to attract top talent. Their recruiting ground is global, with talent for many organizations coming from virtually anywhere through telecommuting. The list of benefits goes on and on.

Internal audit cannot afford to be left behind. Hoss Behzadi believes "the only way for auditors to obtain a seat at the senior management table is through insight and, given the era, more so technology insight." For Martin Silverman, technology is critical to his ability to do his job: "My major job is to provide assurance to the board and executive management that risk is being held to acceptable levels. I can't do it without technology."

Here is what we need from our technology insight: not just specifications for hardware and software, but an ability to take a management view of knowing when to use it and how its use affects the business.

We may not be called on to make the multitude of management decisions relating to securing a new system, but we are charged with helping to ensure that, once the decision is made, the intended outcomes are not hindered by control failures, unrecognized risks, or unexpected organizational culture backlash. Trusted advisors apply their business acumen, industry expertise, and technology insight to such issues and demonstrate the authority and credibility that a broad range of knowledge and skill can inspire.

REMAINING THE STAKEHOLDER'S CONFIDANT

AS I NOTED at the beginning of this book, those trusted advisors who rise to the top of their profession inevitably do so by cultivating a broad portfolio of complementary traits. They don't just show up and articulate their views about how risks can be better managed or the organization can be better controlled without having first earned the trust of those to whom they impart their wisdom. This is true whether the wisdom is imparted as seasoned advice or assurance. Over the course of the book, I have sought to chronicle the portfolio of traits that have been agreed upon by a cadre of CAEs. I started this book firmly convinced of several things:

- Some internal auditors perform in more outstanding ways than others.

- Those internal auditors share a certain set of attributes that enable their outstanding performance. Very few excel in every one of those attributes (even Superman has his kryptonite), but they do demonstrate mastery in a majority of them.

- Those attributes can be grouped into three categories— personal, relational, and professional—that encapsulate what is needed to succeed in internal auditing (and, quite honestly, most other professions).

- Many of those outstanding internal auditors make the leap from outstanding to trusted advisor status.

I still believe those things, although I understand them in a much more profound way than I did when I started my research.

BASIC TRUTHS

One of the joys of working on this book was the opportunity to talk to a number of CAEs about these issues. I was privileged to ask them how they rank the top attributes of outstanding auditors and gain insight as to why. The process was eye-opening. Through a number of follow-up conversations, I came to consider certain issues in a different light. My research made it clear that internal auditors face many of the same challenges that professionals in a wide array of fields deal with on a regular basis. And, finally, I recognize that there are no easy answers and no effortless ways to achieving a measure of success.

I am also even further convinced of a point I made in my first book: internal auditing is not a static profession. I mentioned that the general performance of internal auditors can be displayed in a bell curve—the less motivated or adept are at the left end of the curve, the vast majority settle in the middle, and the superb performers can be found at the right side of the curve. I believe the curve will shift to the right over time as experience and educational tools are made available and exploited. Attributes that are considered "excellent" or "well above average" today will become "prerequisite" and "fundamental" in the future.

If the curve continues to shift to the right, internal auditors need to focus on two key lessons. First, we should be assessing our skills today as a basis for setting ourselves up for success in the future. Second, we need to recognize that the attributes covered in this book will undoubtedly evolve over time and other traits will take their place, or at least be added to them. I don't think the list we've discussed in this book will become irrelevant by any means, but I am convinced it will need adjustment.

We need only to look in the past to know the truth of this. If we transported ourselves back to the 1950s or 1960s and developed a list of the top attributes of outstanding internal auditors practicing at the time, we might include a keen appreciation of accounting, a strong focus on financial reporting, and a dedication to "ticking and tying" on work-papers. Today, in this book, I have not dedicated even a single chapter to those skills. As a profession evolves, the skills needed to excel in it evolve as well. For a more contemporary example, consider that those internal auditors who brought a risk-centric mindset to their work in the 1990s were considered forward thinking. Today, they would simply be meeting the standards.

Technological aptitude was not nearly as important 30 years ago as it is today, at least not in how we view it today. And I think it's reasonable to assume there are technological risks ahead that we cannot even imagine now. Internal auditors who fail to continuously assess their skills and reinvent themselves to align with their current environment will undoubtedly fall short of their potential—and client expectations. As Will Rogers so astutely pointed out, "Even if you're on the right track, you'll get run over if you just sit there."

WHAT THE FUTURE HOLDS

Knowing what the future will bring is hardly an easy task, and I am certainly no fortune-teller. Although I cannot identify the exact attributes that will be required of future trusted advisors, I see some areas that will probably grow in importance.

Emerging risk. Internal auditors will never go wrong by focusing on areas of emerging risk. As business becomes more complex, so do the risks. Understanding threats on and beyond the horizon will help internal auditors define (and develop) the skills that will be needed to address them.

Advocacy. I mention internal auditors' commitment to "ticking and tying" in the 1950s and 1960s. That was also the period when internal auditors were consistently referred to as bean counters or box checkers. I am thankful that those wince-inducing terms are used less often now than they were when I started in the field, but they have not disappeared entirely. When The IIA marked its 75th anniversary in 2016 by ringing the opening bell on the New York Stock Exchange (NYSE), one television commentator referred to us sarcastically as a "really fun bunch." There is a need, and will continue to be a need, to overcome such stereotypes and prove the value of internal audit. We can do that by being advocates—even cheerleaders—for what we do. Waving the flag, as we did at the NYSE, does not make us unprofessional or cheesy. It makes us proactive leaders in the effort to close strategic gaps in the understanding of the need for and importance of internal auditing in business today. If you run into someone who questions that need or importance, ask them if they've ever heard of Enron, WorldCom, or a number of other companies and organizations that more recently tripped on themselves.

Broadened focus. Internal auditors must be willing to acquire the skills and confidence to step outside their comfort zone. A hot topic for internal auditors today is organizational culture. Businesses increasingly recognize the important role culture plays in profitability, compliance, employee satisfaction, and a host of other desirable business factors, and they have also become aware that there are cultural indicators that can be audited. Some internal auditors feel uncomfortable with cultural audits because they can rely more on subjective than objective judgments—historically not a skill encouraged in internal auditing. But it is one we will need to continue to develop even as we work to devise more objective measures to assess against.

Commitment to improvement up and down the organization chart. I believe most internal auditors are committed to the profession. But as we've discussed, this is not a static profession, so getting ahead requires a consistent commitment to self-improvement—and not just for the internal auditor new to the profession. This commitment has to go clear to the top. When I was head of internal review for the U.S. Army, I knew that to have credibility within the organization, I needed to burnish and refine my credentials. I needed to do something to show I was serious about the profession and committed to it. So, though I was already at a senior level in the profession and in the organization, I decided to take The IIA's Certified Internal Auditor (CIA) exam. After hours of dedicated study, I passed it. The IIA recognized the message my achievement conveyed—never ceasing to improve oneself, even when, by most measures, success had been achieved—and sent a senior staff person to an Army conference to present the CIA certificate to me. Although not many people at the executive level take the opportunity to enhance their skills, they should.

In fact, individuals who hold the CIA credential but are not trusted advisors should conduct a forensic analysis to identify which of the characteristics described in this book they are lacking. Are they unapproachable? Not technically knowledgeable? Do they have no sense of the risks their industry is facing? Do others not trust them because their reports reflect no empathy and instead focus on placing blame? CAEs have a special position and should always remember that their shortcomings not only hold them back, they hold their direct reports back and hinder the department's ability to provide value to the company.

STARTING TODAY

As important as it is to our ongoing success to look ahead, we cannot shortchange the value we need to provide today. To that end, we can keep ourselves fully occupied with developing the traits we know we need *now*. While this book reflects my view of those traits and the views of the many senior audit executives I spoke with as part of my research, here are some of the skills the survey respondents noted when they were asked to define what makes internal auditors outstanding:

- "Auditing excellence. Mastering and properly using a large suite of information gathering, assessment, and analysis tools and techniques, as well as project management and methodologies."

- "Providing risk management leadership. Often internal audit is the only source of risk expertise in an organization. While considering potential conflicts, internal audit can still provide leadership."

- "Being facilitative and consultative. Having the ability to facilitate multiple interests, stakeholders, or groups of people to a successful outcome has been very important in my role. In addition, the ability to be consultative in the delivery of our work or mindset has also been important."

- "The ability to navigate between consulting and providing assurance; a willingness to develop solutions *with* the stakeholders."

- "End-to-end process knowledge. One must have a complete understanding of business system integration to properly identify internal controls that matter."

- "Common sense" (cited by several respondents).

- "Understanding the interdependency of system, process, and people and their impact on operations, regulations, and financials."

I'm willing to wager that this list sounds fairly familiar to every internal auditor reading this book. And why not? It's what internal auditors do. When it comes to outstanding internal auditors, the difference is not a matter of what but how. It is not that they do entirely different things; it's that they perform these practices in an outstanding way.

And along the way, they earn trust. They listen to others, they keep their self-interest under control, they display empathy, they share credit, they build relationships, they seek more complete solutions, and they focus on supporting the business. They have their eyes on the future and their feet in the present. Most of all, they cherish and protect the trust they earn, because they are well aware how quickly it can be lost.

FINAL WORDS

James A. Alexander, a consultant with a doctorate in education, has given some thought to the concept of being a trusted advisor in a variety of professions. One trait he points to as setting trusted advisors apart from others in the field is that they tend to be more satisfied with their jobs.[1] If that is the case, then perhaps internal auditing can have no greater advocate than Michael Rosenberg of Och Ziff Capital Management, who offers the most telling indication of job satisfaction: "I like the profession so much, I got my son into it."

I understand and appreciate that degree of commitment to the profession. I have spent almost my entire career in internal auditing and I would never hesitate to encourage someone with the right skills and interests to pursue it as well. I am privileged to lead the world's largest professional association for internal auditors, fully convinced of the value they bring to individual companies and the global economy. Because of that potential impact, I believe we all have a vested interest in ensuring that internal auditors are the best they can be. I have a profound personal sense of obligation to do what I can to help ensure that result.

Throughout my career, and especially in my current role, I have had the opportunity to travel the world and meet internal auditors of all stripes, many of whom are new to the profession. They tend to be very enthusiastic about the field. They seek to learn and improve themselves. My position with The IIA confers a certain credibility on me, and I want to leverage that "bully pulpit," as Teddy Roosevelt would call it, to help those starting out. My hope is that this book will help them become more professional, build a more rewarding career, and enjoy a more prosperous future.

I fervently believe that if you want to become better at something, you study the best in the field and emulate them. Because of my tenure in internal auditing and the amazing exposure I now have to the best in the profession, I can share the wisdom of those trusted advisors. Readers who are striving to understand what it takes to get ahead in internal auditing hopefully found a lot of sage advice on that topic in these pages.

Reading is just the beginning. It must be supported by a continual, focused effort to convert words to actions. Complacency is the enemy of success. Never assume you "have arrived." Keep working at it. When success arrives, embrace it, but continue to look for ways to improve, develop, and evolve.

Internal auditing is not an easy profession. It is often misunderstood and sometimes viewed with condescension and apprehension, even scorn. Dealing with such perceptions can be frustrating, and some people decide to leave the profession for what they hope will be greener pastures. This saddens me. I understand taking a brief sabbatical to explore another field; I did it myself and returned to internal auditing refreshed and with expanded knowledge. However, we cannot afford a permanent brain drain in the profession.

Shortages in the future talent pool are already forecast, and they will only be exacerbated by large-scale exits from the profession. I hope anyone who is considering a permanent career change found material in this book to make them think twice.

We cannot always see the solutions to our own problems. Sometimes we need help perceiving what is right before us. Perhaps you are reading this book because you have hit a wall. Perhaps you have experienced some success, but you see no way clear to break out of your current position. If so, take a long, close look in the mirror and ask yourself if you are functioning at your highest level. If not, take a cue from the outstanding internal auditors who contributed to this book and start down the path toward becoming a trusted advisor. It's a journey you won't regret.

> "We are at our very best, and we are happiest, when we are fully engaged in work we enjoy on the journey toward the goal we've established for ourselves. It gives meaning to our time off and comfort to our sleep. It makes everything else in life so wonderful, so worthwhile."[2]

NOTES

Chapter 1
Key Attributes of Trusted Advisors

1. Jim Collins, *Good to Great: Why Some Companies Make the Leap...And Others Don't* (New York, NY: HarperBusiness, 2001).

Chapter 2
Ethical Resilience

1. Venkataraman Iyer, *CAE Career Paths: Characteristics and Competencies of Today's Internal Audit Leaders* (Lake Mary, FL: The Institute of Internal Auditors Research Foundation, 2016), 12–13.

2. Linda Fisher Thornton, *7 Lenses: Learning the Principles and Practices of Ethical Leadership* (Richmond, VA: Leading in Context LLC, 2013).

3. Chad de Guzman, "Welcome to My Graduation: Mendoza reflects on her term as COA chair," *InterAksyon*, December 20, 2015, http://interaksyon.com/article/121265/welcome-to-my-graduation--mendoza-reflects-on-her-term-as-coa-chair (accessed June 17, 2016).

4. Patricia K. Miller and Larry E. Rittenberg, *The Politics of Internal Auditing* (Lake Mary, FL: Internal Audit Foundation, 2015), 6.

5. Ibid, 54.

Chapter 3
Results Focused

1. *Sawyer's Guide for Internal Auditors, Volume 1, Internal Audit Essentials* (Lake Mary, FL: Internal Audit Foundation, 2012).

2. Matthew Lieberman, "Should Leaders Focus on Results, or on People?" *Harvard Business Review*, December 27, 2013, https://hbr.org/2013/12/should-leaders-focus-on-results-or-on-people (accessed July 17, 2016).

Chapter 4
Intellectually Curious

1. Charles Schwab television commercial, https://www.ispot.tv/ad/7Dai/charles-schwab-why (accessed August 17, 2016).

2. Merriam-Webster, http://www.merriam-webster.com/dictionary/skepticism (accessed July 18, 2016).

3. Aristotle, *Goodreads*, http://www.goodreads.com/quotes/526642-the-more-you-know-the-more-you-know-you-don-t (accessed July 18, 2016).

4. Tomas Chamorro-Premuzic, "Curiosity Is as Important as Intelligence," *Harvard Business Review*, August 27, 2014, https://hbr.org/2014/08/curiosity-is-as-important-as-intelligence/ (accessed July 18, 2016).

5. Ibid.

Chapter 5
Open-Mindedness

1. Annie Murphy Paul, "Why Feeling Confused Will Help You Learn Better," February 15, 2013, http://anniemurphypaul.com/2013/02/why-feeling-confused-will-help-you-learn-better/ (accessed June 16, 2016).

2. Isaac Asimov, *Goodreads*, http://www.goodreads.com/quotes/667214-your-assumptions-are-your-windows-on-the-world-scrub-them (accessed June 16, 2016).

Chapter 6
Dynamic Communicators

1. Amy Rees Anderson, "Successful Business Communication: It Starts at the Beginning," *Forbes*, May 28, 2013, http://www.forbes.com/sites/amyanderson/2013/05/28/successful-business-communication-it-starts-at-the-beginning/#4cf5d88d3280 (accessed June 20, 2016).

2. James Rose, *The Top 7 Skills CAEs Want: Building the Right Mix of Talent for Your Organization* (Lake Mary, FL: The Institute of Internal Auditors Research Foundation, 2016), 1–2.

3. Bernard M. Baruch, *Goodreads*, http://www.goodreads.com/author/quotes/5768330.Bernard_M_Baruch (accessed June 20, 2016).

4. Stephen R. Covey, *Goodreads*, http://www.goodreads.com/quotes/298301-most-people-do-not-listen-with-the-intent-to-understand (accessed June 20, 2016).

5. Amy Rees Anderson, "Successful Business Communication: It Starts at the Beginning."

6. The Institute of Internal Auditors Audit Executive Center, "2016 North American Pulse of Internal Audit: Time to Move Out of the Comfort Zone," 2016, http://contentz.mkt5790.com/lp/2842/201608/2016%20North%20American%20Pulse%20of%20Internal%20Audit%20Report%20%282%29.pdf (accessed June 20, 2016).

7. Jim DeLoach and Charlotta Löfstrand Hjelm, *Six Audit Committee Imperatives: Enabling Internal Audit to Make a Difference* (Lake Mary, FL: The Institute of Internal Auditors Research Foundation, 2016), 6–7.

8. *Ia Magazine*, February 2016, 75th anniversary edition.

Chapter 7
Insightful Relationships

1. Matthew Lieberman, "Should Leaders Focus on Results, or on People?," *Harvard Business Review*, December 27, 2013, https://hbr.org/2013/12/should-leaders-focus-on-results-or-on-people (accessed June 20, 2016).

2. Richard Chambers, *Repairing a Broken Relationship in Your Internal Audit Department*, Chambers on the Profession blog, January 13, 2014, https://iaonline.theiia.org/blogs/chambers/2014/Pages/Repairing-a-Broken-Relationship-in-Your-Internal-Audit-Department.aspx.

3. Richard F. Chambers, Charles B. Eldridge, Paula Park, and Ellen P. Williams, "The relationship advantage: Maximizing chief audit executive success," March 2011, http://www.kornferry.com/institute/317-the-relationship-advantage-maximizing-chief-audit-executive-success (accessed November 18, 2016).

Chapter 8
Inspirational Leaders

1. "Charisma," *Psychology Today*, https://www.psychologytoday.com/basics/charisma (accessed June 21, 2016).

2. Sir Isaac Newton: The Universal Law of Gravitation, http://csep10.phys.utk.edu/astr161/lect/history/newtongrav.html (accessed June 21, 2016).

3. David Biello, "Fact or Fiction?: Archimedes Coined the Term 'Eureka' in the Bath," *Scientific American*, http://www.scientificamerican.com/article/fact-or-fiction-archimede/ (accessed June 21, 2016).

4. Laura Dimon, "Colin Powell's 13 Life Rules For Any Future Leader," *Get Mic Daily*, November 11, 2013, https://mic.com/articles/65663/colin-powell-s-13-life-rules-for-any-future-leader (accessed November 18, 2016).

5. Jack Shafer, "The Tao of Bear," *Slate*, http://www.slate.com/articles/news_and_politics/press_box/2003/05/the_tao_of_bear.html (accessed June 21, 2016).

6. "Nick Saban Makes Fortune's list of 2016 World's Greatest Leaders," March 24, 2016, http://www.rolltide.com/sports/m-footbl/spec-rel/032416aaa.html (accessed June 21, 2016).

7. Cary L. Clark, "Alabama Coach Nick Saban On Win," '*BamaMag*, November 8, 2015, http://www.scout.com/college/alabama/story/1608918-alabama-coach-nick-saban-on-win (accessed June 21, 2016).

8. Quotes Gram, http://quotesgram.com/img/colin-powell-famous-quotes/8923344/ (accessed August 21, 2016).

9. Jack Zenger and Joseph Folkman, "What Inspiring Leaders Do," *Harvard Business Review*, June 20, 2013, https://hbr.org/2013/06/what-inspiring-leaders-do (accessed June 21, 2016).

10. Ibid.

Chapter 9
Critical Thinkers

1. "Defining Critical Thinking," The Critical Thinking Community, http://www.criticalthinking.org/pages/defining-critical-thinking/766 (accessed July 27, 2016).

2. Ibid.

3. Ibid.

4. S. M. Rayhanul Islam, "What are the Importance and Benefits of 'Critical Thinking Skills'?," *LinkedIn*, January 27, 2015, https://www.linkedin.com/pulse/what-importance-benefits-critical-thinking-skills-islam (accessed July 27, 2016).

5. Ibid.

6. Mortimer A. Dittenhofer, Sridhar Ramamoorti, Douglas E. Ziegenfuss, and R. Luke Evans, *Behavioral Dimensions of Internal Auditing: A Practical Guide to Professional Relationships in Internal Auditing* (Lake Mary, FL: Internal Audit Foundation, 2010).

Chapter 10
Technical Expertise

1. Brian Hill, "What Is a Strong General Business Acumen?," *Chron*, http://smallbusiness.chron.com/strong-general-business-acumen-21849.html (accessed July 28, 2016).

Conclusion
Remaining the Stakeholder's Confidant

1. James A. Alexander, "What Trusted Advisors Do That Others Don't," *Top-Consultant*, http://www.top-consultant.com/articles/trustedadvisor.pdf.

2. Earl Nightingale (1921–1989), American author and radio personality.

RESOURCES

MY FIRST BOOK, *Lessons Learned on the Audit Trail*, published by the Internal Audit Foundation, is a good basis for many of the subjects covered in this book, as are my many blog postings (https://iaonline.theiia.org/blogs/chambers). While not an exhaustive list of the sources consulted for this book, the following resources may provide more insight for those who wish to delve further into specific topics.

PERSONAL ATTRIBUTES
Chapter 2
Ethical Resilience

Vivian Giang, "7 Business Leaders Share How They Solved the Biggest Moral Dilemmas of Their Careers," *Fast Company*, June 2, 2015.

Sebastian Bailey, "Business Leaders Beware: Ethical Drift Makes Standards Slip," *Forbes*, May 25, 2013.

"Leadership," *Ethical Systems.org*.

Chapter 3
Results Focused

Matthew Lieberman, "Should Leaders Focus on Results or on People?" *Harvard Business Review*, December 27, 2013.

Senthiyl SSG, "An Unflinching Focus on Results — A Leader's Responsibility," *Arbinger*, January 28, 2015.

Ingar Grev, "5 ways to focus on results instead of process," *The Business Journals*, April 20, 2015.

"The Mindset to Getting Things Done: Think Result-Oriented," *Myrkothum*, December 9, 2008.

Chapter 4
Intellectually Curious

Tomas Chamorro-Premuzic, "Curiosity Is as Important as Intelligence," *Harvard Business Review*, August 27, 2014.

Chapter 5
Open-Mindedness

Annie Murphy Paul, "Why Feeling Confused Will Help You Learn Better," *Anniemurphypaul.com*.

"Authentic Happiness," University of Pennsylvania.

Terri Babers, "Two Essential Leader Qualities," Positive Change Coaching.

David K. Williams, "The 5 Secret Strategies Of Great People: How To Become Open Minded in 2013," *Forbes*, January 7, 2013.

RELATIONAL ATTRIBUTES
Chapter 6
Dynamic Communicators

George N. Root III, "7 C's of Effective Communication," *Chron*.

Scott McLean, Business Communication for Success, v1.0, *Flatworldknowledge.com*, 2016.

Geoffrey James, "The 5 Inviolable Rules for Effective Business Communications," *CBS MoneyWatch*, July 12, 2011.

Chapter 7
Insightful Relationships

Jennifer Miller, "How to Develop a Positive Coaching Relationship with Your Team," *Answers*.

Jim Dougherty, "5 Steps to Building Great Business Relationships," *Harvard Business Review*, December 5, 2014.

Kimberley Laws, "Why Relationships Matter," *Propel Businessworks*, December 22, 2014.

David E. Hawkins, "The importance of relationships," June 2011.

Chapter 8
Inspirational Leaders

Rajesh Patel, "Inspirational Leadership," *Slideshare*, October 27 2009.

Talent Management, "Eight Principles of Inspirational Leadership," February 21, 2013.

Gwen Moran, "Five Keys to Inspiring Leadership, No Matter Your Style," *Entrepreneur*.

Peter Vajda, "How to fail as a leader," *Management.Issues*, August 13, 2013.

PROFESSIONAL ATTRIBUTES
Chapter 9
Critical Thinkers

S. M. Rayhanul Islam, "What are the Importance and Benefits of 'Critical Thinking Skills'?" *LinkedIn*, January 27, 2015.

G. Randy Kasten, "Critical Thinking: A Necessary Skill in the Age of Spin," *Edutopia*, March 2, 2012.

Chapter 10
Technical Expertise

Brian Hill, "What Is a Strong General Business Acumen?" *Chron.*

Lynda Moultry Belcher, "Advantages and Disadvantages of Technology Advances," *Chron.*